DOOF DOOF

Dear Peter

Thank you for the
support you always give
me on Eagle

Simon

SIMON MAY

Doof Doof

MY LIFE IN MUSIC

AUSTIN MACAULEY
PUBLISHERS LTD.

A CIP catalogue record for this title is available from the British Library.

ISBN 9781784555412 (paperback)

www.austinmacauley.com

First Published (2015)

Austin Macauley Publishers Ltd.
25 Canada Square
Canary Wharf
London
E14 5LB

Printed and bound in Great Britain

Dedication

Rosie, Lucy, Olivia, Daisy, Freddie, Nick, Christian and Joe with all my love.

Contents

Preface

'**I**S THAT SIMON May?' I heard this lady's voice on the phone.

'Yes, who's speaking please?'

'I'm a friend of your mother who kindly gave me your phone number. I hope you don't mind me ringing, but we are organizing a special Charity Gala Event in Wiltshire next year and we are looking for a celebrity to open the event.'

As I reached for my diary the voice went on: 'I know you are in the music business, and I wondered if you could help us. Do you know anyone famous?'

I've always accepted that my music is much better known in the UK and other parts of the world than I am.

No surprise then that my announcement to our four children that I was going to write my autobiography was greeted with universal scepticism and reservations.

'Dad, you're a composer, not a writer... Why don't you wait till you retire?... People won't want to read about your life just because you wrote the *EastEnders* theme...' – and other similar words of encouragement!

Thanks to the expertise, talent and experience of my friend Michael Neidus at the Demon Music Group (BBC Worldwide) and the incisive editing skills of Walter

Stephenson at my book publisher Austin Macauley, who have brought some sense and order to my random writing and ramblings, this will hopefully be a story that will interest all lovers of music, television and movies, as well as those who are passionate about education and the future of our young people, and maybe all of you who share the pursuit of happiness.

As this book's subtitle 'My Life in Music' suggests, the chapters of my story are driven by the songs and music I have composed. As such, at various points I have added a small number in the margin, which corresponds to a track number on the 3-CD set of my music that the Demon Music Group (BBC Worldwide) are bringing out in the autumn of 2015. As all of my music and songs trigger different memories and stories at random times during my life, the result is that this autobiography is not in strict chronological order... It is structured more like one of those movies with flashbacks and fast forwards which are often out of sequence.

But why not start with my first piano lesson when I was seven years old?

The First Six Notes...

THE *EASTENDERS* THEME was probably the first tune I started 'composing' when I was seven years old... or at least the first six notes which go up the scale of C major from C to A.

I was seven, she was twenty-one, and it was love at first sight. I remember looking out of the lounge window in Station Road, Devizes, Wiltshire, waiting for my first piano teacher to arrive.

Ann Lake (now Alderman) was young and pretty and from my very first lesson she mentored me and instilled the magic of discovering how to navigate the keys of our modest upright piano. I so looked forward to those lessons because she was friendly and encouraging.

She taught me my first seven notes on the piano, going up the scale of C major. Little did I know that the first six notes of the scale of C major would inspire the opening melody of the *EastEnders* theme thirty-five years later.

My father inherited his father's furniture and house removal firm, F. M. May & Son in Devizes. (We named our son Freddie after my grandfather Frederick.) Our home was an orchard away from the company storage buildings which were opposite the garage where the removal vans were parked overnight.

One of my greatest delights as a nine year old would be to borrow the warehouse key during the weekend and sneak into the massive four-storey building where all the clients' furniture was stored. At any one time there would always be at least ten upright pianos in various parts of the building, most of them unlocked. I would spend hours losing myself in that dark unlit storage building auditioning the different sounds of pianos, some of them so out of tune that they sounded like the pianos that performers like Winifred Atwell and Russ Conway used to play. When I played the Cockney section in the middle of the *EastEnders* theme in a traditional pub 'Russ Conway' style, I think I must have been influenced by those endless hours of playing out of tune pianos in my father's warehouse!

This was my training for the future: experimenting, improvising and playing for hours on end; listening to contrasting sounds coming from different instruments. Today keyboard sounds are refined by digital processors and echo effects. In the 1950s it was less sophisticated, you might say old-fashioned, but the rules don't change. Sonic awareness is an essential skill today for any composer, producer or sound engineer. It's not just about technological skills, it's also about using your ears and recognizing what works and what doesn't.

What I was doing in that dark store room was the equivalent of a young musician today experimenting in their home recording studio, messing about with riffs, hooks, drum loops and voice samples.

I think that my generation has the unique experience of straddling two totally different eras. When I started recording songs at Eden Studios in Kingston upon Thames all we had was a basic two-track analogue tape machine. We learnt how to record a bass guitar the way it would actually sound after being 'bounced' several times (that is, copied from one track to the other as additional instruments were 'overdubbed' onto a new recording). There could be as many as nine or ten 'bounces', which would substantially alter the brightness of the bass from how it sounded on the original 'take'.

Today, digital multi-track facilities are affordable enough for any passionate musician to purchase for use in their own bedroom, and there is no need for all of that. You can simply choose the sound you want for a bass guitar or keyboard and have continuing control over how that will sound, as the track develops and is finally 'mixed'.

In the early days all the music I wrote was handwritten on manuscript paper. Today, thanks to MIDI (Musical Instrument Digital Interface) recording, this is no longer an essential requirement. Musical parts can now be converted and printed from the digital information which has been humanly played into the computer, so that real musicians have got a music score to read and perform.

I WAS not always so fortunate in the allocation of my music teachers as I had been with Ann Lake. My piano teacher at Dauntsey's School was a chain-smoking, rather neurotic elderly man, and in those days it was considered acceptable for a pupil to sit in a tiny room passively inhaling clouds of smoke. Those lessons were a great contrast to my earlier lessons with Ann and may account for the fact that I gave up learning the piano after achieving a modest merit at grade 4.

Also I was useless at sight-reading, which is probably why I eventually decided to become a composer and write my own music!

My violin teacher was no better. He was also a chain-smoker, and rolled up his own brand of tobacco throughout our lessons together. I only made it to grade 2, but I did enjoy playing in the School Orchestra at Dauntsey's School. That gave me my first lesson in understanding the art of orchestration.

Ann Lake was a firm believer in encouraging her pupils to take part in all the local music festivals – for example, in Devizes where my uncle and mother founded and organized the local Eisteddfod, of which I have the honour of being patron to this day. I always try to attend the Festival every year and adjudicate the Composition class as well as having the pleasure of catching up with all my Wiltshire friends like Bruce and Jackie Hopkins, Carole and Chris Berry and the young First Stages performers.

I only won one prize, in the Under-Ten Piano Duet competition in 1953. And I still have a small silver cup which my mother won in the Bath Music Festival, so I guess that's where whatever talent I have came from. Not from my dear father, sadly: he was tone-deaf and followed the *English Hymnal* in Chapel every Sunday, but never opened his mouth to sing!

I remember how nervous I was playing at those music festivals. I still recall my pounding heart and clammy hands as I waited for my turn to perform in front of the other competitors, wishing that I was at home watching the next episode of *The Lone Ranger*!

Over the years I have learnt how to overcome my nerves. The secret, which I have shared with our children Lucy, Olivia, Daisy and Freddie, is to imagine a worse scenario. Whenever our children were about to take a dreaded exam I told them to imagine they were waiting in the dental surgery, about to have four teeth extracted by an unskilled dentist without an anaesthetic. What could be worse? Taking an exam for which they had prepared was surely nothing to get worked up about!

At least that was the theory. Although I have learnt how to handle television and radio interviews and to speak in public, nerves do still occasionally get the better of me. To give you one of the more embarrassing examples:

In 1987, my wife Rosie and I went to the Grosvenor House Hotel in London where I was to receive the TRIC (Television and Radio) Award for the *Howards' Way* ② theme. The producer of *Howard's Way* Gerald Glaister and his wife Joan joined us at the luncheon table. Not that I could eat any lunch, because I was petrified that I would forget my rehearsed short acceptance speech.

The award winners before me included the legendary Sir David Frost, Bob Monkhouse and an assembly of highly experienced and professional media figures whose words fell from the tongue with graceful ease and whose speeches were surely going to make mine seem dreary and amateur.

I had written down and gone over countless times what I was going to say. During the lunch I made several visits to the cloakroom to rehearse a final run-through:

'I would like to thank my producer Gerry Glaister who has always believed in me and given me the opportunities to write famous pieces of music for his drama series. Without Gerry as my patron it would not have been possible for me to have had a successful career and enjoy supporting my wife and children…'

Well of course, by the time I was up on the stage receiving my award from Sir David, I had lost it and all I could do was blurt out:

'Thank you, ladies and gentlemen. I would like to say that without Gerry Glaister it would not have been possible for me and my wife to have children!'

Gales of laughter followed from the thousand or so guests, and the following award recipients proceeded in jest to thank Gerry also for making their awards possible. Gerry was a dapper, diminutive gentleman (an ex-RAF pilot), but for the rest of the ceremony he stood very tall and seemed very pleased with his new-found reputation.

The *Howards' Way* main theme had been written in a concentrated one-hour session. The arrangement (orchestration) took a lot longer with the highly skilful talent of the late, dear Ian Hughes like the other versions crafted with my other collaborators Simon Lockyer, Brad and Stu James and Dave Hewson...

I did warn you earlier that I wouldn't always be telling you my story in chronological order, so please bear with me for that 'fast forward'! Before I go on to tell you how *Howards' Way* and *EastEnders* happened in my golden year of 1986, let me go back to my childhood again and explain how I believe I was destined to become a professional composer. I truly believe that all the good stuff that happens in our lives is 'meant to be'.

MY BROTHER Michael and I were very close to my mother's parents 'Nan' and 'Tip'. (I was the one to re-christen my grandad when I was very young, 'Tip' being short for 'typical'!) Summer holidays spent with them near Barnstaple in North Devon were always happy times. And that love of the sea has always stayed with me, which is why I was so excited when Gerry asked me to write the music for *Howards' Way*.

In the 1950s, travelling from Wiltshire to Devon was at least a five-hour-long car journey without a radio or heating. Blankets were needed in the back seat. It wasn't exactly coach and horses, although cars in those days were still measured by their 'horse power'. Climbing Porlock Hill from Lynmouth to Lynton was a scary experience in our little, black, four-horsepower Morris. There was always an element of uncertainty as to whether we would make it to the top of the hill without the engine overheating or the gear slipping.

However, we would always get by and if necessary improvise to reach the top of the steep hill. That would sometimes necessitate me, being the youngest, getting out of the car and walking up the hill to reduce the load. Maybe those experiences influenced the lyrics in my musical *Smike*: 'People think they see a mountain, but it's just a little hill.'

All I know is that those summer holidays in Devon were so happily spent with my parents, brother and grandparents. And many years later, in 1970, I was devastated when my grandmother passed away and I had my first profound experience of bereavement.

I had a very happy childhood. Michael and I would spend hours in F. M. May & Son's spacious storage yard. The brick walls made excellent fielders for our cricket matches played on the backyard concrete surface between the garage and the buildings. And we would spend hours practising tennis shots against the vast 'practice area'. I was lucky enough to be selected for the Wiltshire junior tennis team which I put down to those hours of trying to beat an unpredictable, rough, brick wall – oh, and also to some very helpful coaching from the legendary 'Voice of Wimbledon' Dan Maskell when I used to go to Torquay for coaching weeks sponsored by the Lawn Tennis Association.

Lord Andrew Lloyd Webber apparently used to play with his home toy theatre, and we all know what happened to those childhood dreams.

I had a not dissimilar rehearsal for the real thing by creating my own radio station at home. Three good friends – Jeremy Leonard and Sheila and Linda Carey – would come round and we would record our own songs on a 3¾ inch-per-second tape machine. No such things as a digital 'drop-in' to correct a mistake. If anything was performed badly (and it usually was!), we would have to go through the whole piece again. My long-suffering mother would have to endure the same song up to fifty times a morning while we tried to get it right.

I would then broadcast the 'record' with my DJ voice-over via a long hose from our vacuum cleaner pushed under the playroom door into the lounge. My listening figures weren't too good, in fact my most loyal listener was our golden cocker spaniel Prince who would stare at the end of the hose, head cocked and inquisitively sniffing at this strange sound coming from the playroom.

All of these childhood memories still remain vivid today, and I mention them because they tell the story about apprenticeship and training. If my brother and I hadn't played with our farm set for hours and hours pretending to be the different voices of all the animals, or if I hadn't spent hours performing those excruciatingly bad pop songs with my mates, I am certain that my adult passion for – indeed, obsession with – words, theatre and music would not have followed.

I believe that most of today's young people, fortunately, have survived the techno society we live in. Although some have had their imagination and creativity stunted by passive entertainment from TV and PlayStations, there are just as many who are excited about writing their own music or poetry, or who yearn to become performing artists, professional athletes or creative entrepreneurs in so many different ways.

Our daughter Daisy is one of them. She studied to be an actor at 'ArtsEd' (Arts Educational Schools London) in Chiswick and loved every minute of it. She has appeared in ITV dramas *Lewis* and *Whitechapel* and in 2014 played Celia in the Shakespeare Tobacco Company's touring production of *As You Like It*, for which she was later nominated in the prestigious Ian Charleson Awards.

FRIENDS SOMETIMES tell me they envy me being able to play the piano and improvise. It's a nice compliment, but there is a simple explanation why I can play and compose the way I do: it's rather like that comment by golfer Gary Player, who explained that the more he practised the 'luckier' he got.

I am often asked how I compose music. You've probably heard the story of the late American lyricist Sammy Cahn who was asked: 'Which comes first, the music or the lyrics?' 'The phone call,' he replied.

It is also about improvising and capturing those magical moments when the improvisation becomes memorable and creates an unforgettable emotional impression. Some eminent scientists have described it as a relaxed moment of absorption when the creative mind 'goes with the flow'.

I remember so well the very first time I performed my first meaningful improvisation. I'm not sure exactly how old I was, but I had just bought the sheet music of 'Someday My Prince Will Come' from the Disney film *Snow White and The Seven Dwarfs*. I've never been good at reading music. (The sight-reading part of my piano examinations used to scare the life out of me.) I couldn't play what was on the sheet music, so I started to work out what the basic chords were and then move the fingers of my right hand around to create a new melody over the original chord sequence. It was a magical and exciting discovery that I could create my own tunes!

I have learnt since then that there are only so many great chord sequences that work really well. Ask Gary Barlow what they are. He's used every one of them, which is why he's such a great 'pop' writer. If you've read his autobiography you will learn that his experience of playing other composers' songs in clubs taught him the rules of the game.

There are only seven notes on a piano. Well, that's not strictly true. What I mean is that if you play a major scale in the simplest key of C major, there are only seven white notes (also available in higher or lower octaves). There are also five black notes in each octave (sharps and flats... or Kit Kats, as one of my Asperger music students calls them!), so a purist would correctly tell you that there are in fact twelve notes in every octave on a keyboard. When I sketched *EastEnders* in its original key of C, however, I only used the seven white ones.

Although seven or say twelve possible notes do offer a composer lots of different combinations, nevertheless when you write a tune that sounds so simple and direct, you always fear that it has a rather familiar ring to it and has perhaps been 'stolen' from another piece of music. I have rarely had a problem with plagiarism because I have such a poor memory and can never recall exactly what another composer has written. My collaborators Simon Lockyer, John Brant and I often joke about that 'dyslexic' melody that sounds hauntingly familiar but which fortunately isn't an exact replica of the original piece which may have subliminally prompted its inspiration.

There is a mistaken view that in law plagiarism is defined by seven notes being identical. I learnt several years ago from the eminent musicologist Peter Oxendale that this is not the case. Plagiarism can be claimed if it can be proved that a song or piece of music could not have been written were it not for the existence and awareness of the original piece. Awareness is an important consideration. If Robinson Crusoe had written the melody of 'She Loves You' on his desert island he couldn't have been sued. Any composer in the world born after the nineteen-sixties would not be so lucky.

Don't Let Life Get You Down

ARE OUR ACCOMPLISHMENTS the result of our genes or our experience? A much-asked question to which there is no absolute answer. Of course we inherit the DNA of our parents and grandparents, but I am inclined to believe that our experiences count for more. Which is why I have always passionately believed in education.

When I was ten, if I hadn't watched a very talented Latin teacher playing Rachmaninov and Chopin at my prep school just before bedtime for hours on end (even though he did have a revolting habit of taking snuff in between each movement), or hero-worshipped a senior sixth former at boarding school who would improvise in the practice rooms in front of a dozen other awestruck juniors, watching the way his fingers grabbed notes out of nowhere as he created chord sequences and melodies of his own, would I have written *Howards' Way* and *EastEnders*? I doubt it, whatever genes I had been given.

Would I have got a Choral Scholarship to Corpus Christi College, Cambridge, if Philippe Oboussier and Jim Hodges, the Heads of Music and Drama at Dauntsey's School, hadn't been insane devotees of Mozart and given me the tenor roles in *Cosi Fan Tutte*, *The Marriage of Figaro* and other operas which the school performed annually?

I don't think so.

Which is why much of the music I have composed in my life has such a big connection with education and working with young people.

After prep school and an enjoyable five years at Dauntsey's I studied Modern Languages at Cambridge University. I'd like to say it was the happiest period of my life, but it wasn't really, especially the first year when I was younger than most of my contemporaries.

Being awarded a Choral Scholarship at Cambridge has special memories for me, however. Before my A-Level results came through, Philippe Obousier arranged for me to go to King's College Cambridge, who were auditioning tenor and bass choristers for their group of colleges, which included Corpus Christi.

Richard Armstrong, the organ scholar at Corpus, greeted a rather nervous me with a smile and warm handshake. An organ scholar in his second year, he was responsible not only for playing organ at all the college chapel services, but also for rehearsing and conducting the choir of tenors and basses... as well as choosing the new intake of choral exhibitioners for the following year.

I sang an aria from Handel's *Messiah* in the vast, dark and empty King's College Chapel, which in itself was quite an experience – and then went back to Corpus for a sightreading test with Richard.

I also met the Corpus Tutor, Michael McCrum (who later went on to become Headmaster of Eton College before returning to Corpus as Master). I had been warned that if you wanted to pass the McCrum interview he would suddenly throw a waste paper basket at you. If you dropped it, you failed. If you caught it, you were awarded a place, but if you passed it back to him like an accomplished fly half and showed yourself as a potential player for the college rugby team, you got a scholarship! That never happened, but we had a friendly conversation.

A week later I was having breakfast in the Dauntsey's School noisy dining room, when one of the teachers came to our table, where I was chatting to Nigel Smith, who was at the time singing the lead baritone role in the School production of *Cosi Fan Tutte*. (I was performing the tenor part of Ferrando.)

'Simon, you've got a telegram!'

I opened it. 'Many congratulations on your Choral Exhibition to Corpus Christi!'

OMG (we didn't say that then!) … I was ecstatic. I hadn't even got my A-Level results, and when they did arrive, they were low grade passes. But that didn't matter. Today a Choral Scholarship can only be awarded to an applicant who has already got amazing grades and passed a stringent interview. In those days a choral scholarship could be your entrée to Oxbridge. You didn't need to work or even talk your way in. I sung my way into Cambridge!

In return for an annual £40 exhibition bursary I was required to attend three choir rehearsals a week and get up early every Sunday morning to sing in Communion and later in the day at Evensong.

We performed anthems, Magnificats and psalms to a very high and demanding level of accomplishment.

Sightreading vocal parts was challenging, but a lot easier than playing a full piano score – and it helped me later when I was auditioning to sing in the vocal group Rain. Destiny!

Richard (now Sir Richard) Armstrong went on to become conductor at Welsh National Opera and has since enjoyed a very prestigious career. In choir I sang next to John Cameron who became one of the most successful orchestral arrangers of West End musicals. I wrote for the Cambridge newspaper *Varsity* and met many leading politicians of the day when they visited the University. And there were many other undergraduate friends who later pursued eminent careers in government, the arts, the civil service and commerce.

But I was a small fish in a big pond. It was only after I left Cambridge that I valued it so highly. I returned recently to a College reunion and had the pleasure of chatting to journalist Simon Heffer and several other distinguished alumni and we agreed how special Cambridge had been for us.

In those days, Cambridge students had to wear gowns at all times, even when going out at night to clubs and cinemas. If a University proctor challenged you without a gown, you had to do the honourable thing and reveal your identity and receive a fine. If you were not back in college by 11 p.m. the gates were locked and you had to wake up the porter and be 'gated'. How times have changed!

After getting a third class honours degree at Cambridge (which I put down more to my mild dyslexia and bad memory than laziness), I took a year's Diploma of Education course at Reading University. And then I successfully applied for a teaching post at Kingston Grammar School (KGS) in Surrey.

The seven years I taught there were happy times. I still keep in touch with former students, two of whom (Alan and Mick) are godparents to Lucy and Olivia, our eldest daughters.

I have always enjoyed working with young people and still do. I taught games three afternoons a week, hockey, cricket and tennis. The KGS sports fields were by the River Thames, opposite the grounds of Hampton Court Palace. The school was and remains one of the top hockey schools in the UK. Coaching the Under 12 cricket team was always fun. Your team could be bowled out for under twenty runs but there was still a good chance of winning the match.

When I wasn't marking homework or preparing lessons, I kept writing songs in my spare time. During the weekends and school holidays I would travel to Wiltshire to rehearse and record new songs with Roger Holman and Chaz Hary who had been members of our original group The Dominant Sect, a five-piece pop group with Rick Wells on bass, Adrian Hailstone on drums, Chaz and Roger on guitars and me on lead vocals. We played live gigs in Wiltshire during my student days, but due to our changing circumstances Roger, Chaz and I reformed to become Simon Plug & Grimes. Don't ask me how we came to choose that name!

I can't remember exactly how we got our first recording contract with Decca Records. We tried unsuccessfully to get a meeting with Dick Rowe, the Head of A&R ('Artists and Repertoire'), and I wasted hours waiting in the ground floor reception of Decca Buildings along the London Embankment for a provisional meeting that never happened.

Our breakthrough came after we found a friendly manager, Mark Joseph, who secured a record deal for us with Decca, helped no doubt by a publicity stunt in which Mark smuggled a framed painting of our group into the National Portrait Gallery. The *Daily Express* took a sneak photo of the three of us standing in front of our portrait before it was hastily removed by Security. We made the front page headlines in the *Express*, and Decca signed us shortly afterwards for a three year deal with an 'advance' of £100k – a slightly misleading figure, as I think we only received £5,000 between us and the balance of £95,000 was, if I remember correctly, only payable if we had three top ten singles, which never happened! Anyway it is worth noting here that Decca turned down the Beatles and signed Simon Plug & Grimes!

1970 NOT only brought the deep sadness of my grandmother's death. Something else happened later that was to challenge and change my life.

I was playing hockey on a Saturday afternoon on the KGS playing fields and suddenly, without any warning, my back went into a state of spasm. I couldn't move and had to be carried off the field.

I ended up in hospital for three months. In those days a 'slipped disc', as it was then called, was treated by immobility, sedation and traction. For weeks on end I lay in bed in hospital with weights attached to my feet to keep me stretched out. The school was a kind employer and I was on paid sick leave for all those weeks.

When I finally returned to school I postponed my plans to move to another school and seek promotion. I was a Housemaster at KGS but not Head of Department and I had planned to move on. That would have seemed very ungrateful and disloyal after the school had held my teaching post for three months.

That pivotal setback was probably the reason I became a professional songwriter and composer. Instead of furthering my career as a teacher, I decided to stay at KGS for at least another full academic year.

The Director of Music at KGS was on a different planet to the kids. He didn't really like me because he knew I loved music. That sounds a dreadful thing to say, but it's true. When the Headmaster called me into his office and asked me to bolster the music department and form a new school choir, the Head of Music's dislike for me turned into undisguised hostility.

All teachers are familiar with the infighting and politics that happen in every staff room. The Director of Music decided that my music sessions in the school hall were a non-starter and that the grand piano would remain locked and used for morning assemblies and his music lessons only.

So I recruited new singers to join a music project in the Art Room which unusually had a ropey, old, upright piano in the corner which Denis the art teacher kindly said I could use in lunch breaks.

The first session was dreadful. The kids couldn't sing. I think they only came because they quite liked me and were curious as to what was on offer. I tried teaching them a bit of music theory, but it wasn't working.

At the end of the first lunchtime session, I announced that the lesson had been a disaster and that I was going to write a musical for them to perform at the end of the summer term.

What had I committed myself to? That new musical didn't exist and I had to write it.

This was like Sammy Cahn's phone call. I believe all music has to be written for an occasion, whether it's an artist or band writing for their next album or a composer deadlined to write for a new movie... or Mozart being commissioned to write for the next State Wedding or Funeral in Salzburg or Vienna. Just as our song 'All of Me' was recorded by Blake for release at the time of the Royal Wedding in 2011.

I can't remember what gave me the idea of *Smike* but I've always been a great fan of Charles Dickens and in 1972 *Nicholas Nickleby* was still open territory, unlike *Oliver Twist*, which had been comprehensively colonised by Lionel Bart's smash-hit musical *Oliver*.

In the second of those lunch-break music sessions I played the boys my first song from *Smike*. As you may have already gathered from reading the first pages of my story, I don't worry too much about keeping everything in chronological order. I instinctively go with whatever comes to mind first. And I knew that my first key song in *Smike* would address the heart of the musical and come at the end of Act One. 'Don't Let Life Get You Down' is a ③ message of hope and comfort given by the newly arrived teacher at Dotheboys Hall, Nicholas Nickleby, and sung to the abused orphan Smike who has just received a beating from Mr Squeers, the violent and bullying headmaster.

As early as week one of writing the musical, the universal theme of abuse and bullying was already taking shape, and my optimistic belief in the kindness and resilience shown by Nicholas Nickleby was already expressed in my lyrics. *'If you think that you're a loser, you're never going to win,'* Nicholas sings to Smike. Was that a foretaste of another lyric 'Every Loser Wins' which I co-wrote thirteen years later for EastEnders?

I have to say that as I played and sang 'Don't Let Life Get You Down' for the first time in that Art Room lunchbreak session, you could hear a pin drop. I finished singing and looked up rather nervously, waiting for the boys' reaction... they loved it, and I thank them to this day for their enthusiastic and positive response which inspired me to continue the journey. As the story of *Smike* developed, I would write a new song each week and give the boys a reason to sing.

The students I was working with were bright, talented and open-minded. Amongst them were Neil Fox (future DJ and TV presenter) and Richard Dodds (future captain of the GB Hockey eleven who won Gold in the Seoul Olympics in 1986). All the other boys were premier league too and went on to enjoy very successful careers after KGS.

At the same time, Roger Holman and I had just signed an exclusive songwriting contract with Geoffrey Heath and Eddie Levy at ATV Music. The publishing company owned the Lennon/McCartney catalogue as well as publishing writers like Barry Blue, Lynsey de Paul, Tony Hiller (co-writer of the Brotherhood of Man's Eurovision-winning song 'Save Your Kisses for Me'), and many others. The advance of £1000 per year was not enough to support us both, so Roger went full time as professional songwriter and I remained teaching for at least the rest of that year with a view to *Smike* being a kind of 'swansong' before I also went full time pro the following year.

Writing *Smike* was such fun. History teacher Clive Barnett and I spent a week during the holidays adapting the dialogue from the Dotheboys Hall sequence of *Nicholas Nickleby* and interpolating it into our script. Roger helped me with the arrangements of the music. I am sure, however, that they would be gracious enough to agree that the show was my 'baby' and my baptism of fire. My future best man and great friend Steve Elson played guitar in the performances at Surbiton Assembly Rooms. Steve is now lead singer of the very successful tribute band The Counterfeit Stones. I have to thank him, all the musicians and the *whole* production team who contributed to the show's success, including dear Lorraine Clarke my choreographer and the local girls' schools who added a feminine touch to the cast!

For the first time in my life, I realized that I could write tunes and lyrics that everyone would be humming for the next few minutes, hours, days and maybe longer!

The first performance of *Smike* at Surbiton Assembly Rooms caused a massive stir locally and further afield. Monica Sims, the Head of BBC TV Children's Department, asked me to adapt the show with producer Paul Ciani into a 50-minute Christmas Special.

By then I had given in my notice to KGS, resigning in the summer of 1973. But I wouldn't be saying goodbye to my 'Smike' kids. They were to appear in the BBC production, although the lead part of Smike was to be performed by Ian Sharrock, an engaging youngster from the Corona Stage School. The role of Smike was one of Ian's first major acting roles. He went on to play Jackie Merrick in *Emmerdale Farm* and we became good friends during the pre-production and making of the TV special. Leonard Whiting, who played Romeo in Zeffirelli's magical film version of *Romeo and Juliet*, and the great Beryl Reid starred in the BBC TV production. I was becoming a fully-fledged songwriter and composer!

Smike has become a mini-classic, performed by thousands of schools and amateur dramatic societies in the UK and overseas. At the end of this book, I have listed all the schools and amateur dramatic societies whose recent productions of *Smike* I have enjoyed watching. I have tried to recall as many names that I can of all the producers and music directors I have personally met and got to know over the years (sometimes during the course of a *Smike* seminar ahead of their performances). Since 1974, I have had the fun of meeting many thousands of youngsters who have performed *Smike*, and I hope they remember me with as much collective affection as I still have for them. Such happy memories!

During my last years at KGS I was also enjoying that first record deal with Decca Records. This is the first defini-tive time that I realized the power of positive thinking, of my inability to understand the word 'No'. When I was giving spelling lessons at the Park School in Woking until five years ago I used to teach them that NO is spelt Y...E...S...! Cheesy? Yes, but so useful to know!

Our second single as Simon Plug & Grimes was released in late 1970. It got one spin on Radio 1 and then... nothing. One afternoon after school, I drove from Kingston upon Thames to Shepherds Bush and marched into BBC Television Centre on a mission. Security was lax in those days, and I ignored main reception and caught the lift to the sixth-floor Light Entertainment offices.

The first office I came across was marked 'Basil Brush Show'. This was the prime L.E. (Light Entertainment) spot on the Beeb, with higher ratings than the lottery show or *X Factor* today. The producer's name was on the door – Johnny Downes.

I knocked and walked in. I smiled at the secretary in the outer office and announced myself as the lead singer in the pop group Simon Plug & Grimes.

'Is it possible to give a copy of our single to Mr Downes, please?' I asked her.

'I'm afraid Mr Downes is busy and can't see you without an appointment,' she replied rather sternly.

As fate would have it, two other phones started ringing on her desk and whilst she was distracted I moved to the half-open door of Johnny Downes' inner office and walked in without fear.

'Hello Mr Downes,' I said to the unsuspecting producer. He had just finished a phone conversation and looked up at me rather bemused. 'I am Simon May and I'm the singer in a new group who would like to be on your show.'

Whether my innocent and youthful look caught him at the right moment or whether he took pity on me I'll never know, but for whatever reason he allowed me to tell him about our band and how good the record was and how right it would be for his show, and there I was putting the 45 record on his turntable playing him 'Way In Way Out', which was a tuneful, upbeat, feelgood song about nothing in particular.

'Simon, thank you for coming to see me. I'll keep you in mind' said Johnny. 'Now I have work to do, so would you mind letting yourself out please?'

'May I leave you my telephone number, Mr Downes? I know we'd be great on your show, and I look forward to hearing from you soon,' I managed to get in before the rather amused but 'pissed off' secretary came in to usher me away.

I returned home to my digs in Kingston. And this is the absolute truth, I had just started cooking my supper when the phone rang: 'Hello Simon, this is Johnny Downes's office. He would like to speak to you,' a voice said.

I was trembling. 'Simon, this is Johnny Downes. We all love your record. We've just had a cancellation for this Saturday. Are you available to come on the show?'

Were we available? Wow! That's the stuff dreams are made of. I couldn't believe our luck...

Roger, Chaz and I were at Television Centre a few days later making our television debut on BBC TV. Decca Records Promotion Department couldn't get their heads round how I had got the slot. The record started selling a few and getting airplay, but the day after the TV show was transmitted, local sales in Kingston soared, mainly due to the rapturous reception it had received from my pupils! In fact, at HMV Kingston it was the number one selling single of the week, and Carol the manager of the store and I became good friends. Roger, Chaz and I attended a local personal appearance 'in store' which was covered by the local press and radio and for a brief moment I thought we had made it.

A couple of weeks later I popped in to have a coffee with Carol. 'How's the record doing?' I asked her. She looked at me rather awkwardly. 'Well Simon, yesterday we sold one copy, but today hasn't been quite so busy!'

I TRUST I'm not boring you with all of this. I was foolish enough to ask the same question at the Park School, where I used to teach, after beginning a talk about metaphors and similes.

'Am I boring you?' I asked ten minutes into the lesson.

'Not yet!' came a voice from the back.

Our first pay cheque from the BBC which I couldn't bear to encash!

Born with a Smile on My Face

MY GRANDMOTHER (ON my mother's side) gave my brother Michael and me unconditional love. She adored us and we adored her. Like all grandparents, she and my grandfather 'Tip' had the benefits of a close relationship without responsibility. Sir Cliff Richard (and I'll tell you about our friendship later in the story) always talks about the fun and love he has with his nephews and nieces. 'But they always go away!' he jokes. And I can understand that. With your own children there is always homework, revision, health and practical issues to nag them about.

My grandmother 'Nan' was never judgemental, and always our number one fan. One of her biggest pleasures was watching *Crossroads* and one of my deepest regrets is that my string of hit records featured on *Crossroads* began four years after she died. Or maybe she was watching over me helping to create that success from above. If she did, she certainly chose her favourite programme as a launching pad for my career as a songwriter.

She died of cancer in 1970. Only my mother and father went to the funeral and whilst I respected their wishes, I do sometimes wish I was given the chance to say goodbye.

Whilst *Smike* was moving forwards, Roger and I were getting to know the A&R department at ATV music and writing songs for them to promote.

In early 1974, after I had left Kingston Grammar School, I was in our publisher's office in Mayfair when Len Beadle, one of the A&R executives, popped into the writers' area and said: 'ATV *Crossroads* want a fifteen-second extract of a song to use in a background sequence. All songs to me, please, by tomorrow morning.'

Well, that's not a great deal to get excited about. And none of the writers did anything… except me. I gave Len a copy of an old song which Roger had written with me a year ago and which had been rejected by comedian Jimmy Tarbuck, called 'Born with a Smile on My Face'. ④ (A song driven more by Roger than me, actually.)

'Thanks Simon,' said Len. 'You're the only writer who has given me something to send to Birmingham.'

Two days later I received a phone call from Jack Barton, Producer of *Crossroads*.

'Hello Simon, we haven't met, but last year my wife Yvonne and I so enjoyed your musical *Smike* at Surbiton Assembly Rooms.' (It turned out they lived two miles away from Surbiton, in Thames Ditton.) 'I've just received your song "Born with a Smile on My Face". I like the singer's voice. Stephanie de Sykes… is she pretty?'

Is the Pope Catholic? I could see something stirring here, and Jack and I agreed to meet up. At the same time Len Beadle, who had been one of the four singers in the very successful harmony group The Raindrops, had auditioned for four young singers to be in his new reformed band, to be known as Rain.

Stephanie and I met during auditions, and because of my choral background in Cambridge, reading vocal parts and performing intricate harmonies wasn't too much of a problem for me. So alongside Chaz and Alex, I was chosen to be one of the lucky three male singers to back Stephanie in the pop group known as Stephanie de Sykes and Rain.

What none of us realized at the time was that Jack, a veteran lover of music hall theatre and showbiz, was going to extend the fifteen-second sequence of 'Born with a Smile' and create a major storyline about a 'famous' pop singer who dropped into the Crossroads Motel for a week to escape from showbiz pressures.

How Jack managed to plug the song relentlessly on one of the highest rating TV soaps in the UK was an exciting revelation to me, which would put even Simon Cowell to shame today!

Stephanie was engaged as an actor to appear in the show for a four-week run. The rest, as they say, is history.

When 'Born with a Smile on My Face' was first released in 1974, I sent a copy to one of my producer mates at Radio 1, the late Tony Fish, who later became manager of BBC Radio Newcastle and then Editor of BBC Radio Shropshire. Tony had been one of my favourite pupils at Kingston Grammar School in the 1960s.

'Tony, any chance of a spin for "Born with a Smile"…?'

'Sorry Si, that will never get played on Radio 1.'

After two weeks of exposure on *Crossroads*, the record leapt into the Charts at Number 14 and went up to Number 2 in the following week...

'Simon, it's Tony here. We haven't got a copy of "Born with a Smile" and we need it for the chart run-down on Sunday. Could you possibly get me a copy over?'

'Go and buy one, Tony,' I replied.

Stephanie and Rain went on tour for several months on the back of 'Born with a Smile on My Face'. We performed at Batley Variety Club, Lakeside and many other popular 'cabaret' venues in the UK. I still have such a happy memory of my mother and father coming to see us perform at the Savoy, which gave me the chance of treating them to a weekend break in London.

During that year, we also recorded Lynsey de Paul's theme song for the popular ITV show *The Golden Shot*, hosted by the iconic Bob Monkhouse. Whenever I speak at after dinner events, I have always taken Mr Monkhouse as my guide on how to speak 'off the cuff'. He concealed his skill brilliantly. All his seemingly effortless ad libs were cleverly scripted, rehearsed and perfected.

After 'Born with a Smile on My Face', Jack Barton and I had great fun plugging songs on *Crossroads*, all of which, to the great irritation of some radio executives and DJs, became big hits in the UK: 'We'll Find Our Day' (the parody love song from *Smike*) which Stephanie de Sykes came back to perform at Meg Richardson's *Crossroads* wedding... and 'Benny's Theme': an interesting instrumental piece musically, but the butt of much media ridicule because of Benny's over-the-top, spoken voice-over.

(7)   'More Than In Love' was another big hit record which was featured on *Crossroads*. It was performed by the beautiful and talented Kate Robbins. Jack Barton created a storyline about a singer on tour having a love affair with one of the soap's leading actors, Adam Chance. Somehow Jack managed to introduce a recording studio in the basement of the Crossroads Motel where the song was 'recorded'!

The record got to Number 2 in the UK charts in 1981. Without *Crossroads* it wouldn't have enjoyed the success that it did. But this is true of many of the hit records that have emanated from the Simon Cowell hit factory with *Britain's Got Talent* and *The X Factor* today. Hey Simon, we enjoyed using the power of television to make hit records years ago!

But most importantly in 1976… this was the year that I met my darling wife Rosie. It was 'The Summer of My Life'.

The Summer of My Life

I HAD WRITTEN 'THE Summer of My Life' before I ⑤ fell in love with Rosie. But it's a much better story to embellish it by saying that I wrote it for her. Well, maybe I did, because I've always tried to be ahead of my time and look into the future! Whatever actually happened, I can't remember the details, but the song became our love song and will always remain so.

Rosie worked as receptionist at ATV Music when I first met her. We exchanged friendly conversations and I found her very attractive. She was pretty and engaging but I didn't realize at that early stage how much she was going to mean to me for the rest of my life. I had another girlfriend at the time and wasn't looking for another romance. I was also very focused on my music. Things were going well and I had plans for my future songwriting career.

A few months later, though, we started dating. We spent a happy first day together by the coast in Dorset. Gradually the large bedroom wardrobe of my Hampton Court bachelor home seemed to contain fewer of my clothes to make room for hers!

She moved in and became part of that hot summer of my life in 1976. I invited her to spend a weekend with me at my parents' cottage in Wiltshire. My mother knew before I did that she was the one for me.

On lazy Sunday afternoons spent with Jack Barton, his dear wife Yvonne and daughter Nicolette, the two of us would talk show business and music. Jack was a very private person. He would spend the week in Birmingham ruling the *Crossroads* set with a rod of iron – just as Julia Smith, producer of *EastEnders*, did ten years later in Elstree. But on a Sunday I was the only privileged friend whom Jack and his family were happy to spend time with. Yvonne enjoyed my friendship with Jack vicariously. Sadly Jack and Yvonne have passed away, but Rosie, I and the family still enjoy a warm and continuing friendship with Nicolette, who is godmother to our daughter Olivia.

On one of those Sunday afternoons in early 1976, Jack hit me with a new storyline for *Crossroads*. It was about a love triangle romance between a man and the two women in his life which culminated in sad unrequited love. 'Write me a song that tells the story,' said Jack.

So I did. 'Summer of My Life' was a love song which broke the rules of the normal pop format: like 'Eloise' by Barry Ryan and 'Music Was My First Love' by John Miles, it enjoyed an indulgent orchestral development section.

After I had composed the piece I travelled to Birmingham and performed the song to Jack in the vast Studio One at ATV Studios, which was the only place with a piano – a magnificent grand used by Johnny Patrick and the ATV Orchestra in shows like *New Faces*, with its hit theme tune 'You're a Star'. This was a talent show judged by celebrities of the day, such as *Crossroads* and *Neighbours* composer Tony Hatch who was the first to show how to be 'Mr Nasty'… something which Simon Cowell has copied so successfully in his shows *Pop Idol*, *The X Factor* and *Britain's Got Talent*.

After I had sung and played 'Summer of My Life' to Jack, I was relieved to see that he shared my excitement. 'Who do you think should perform this?' asked Jack. I hesitated for less than a second and replied: 'Could I do it please, Jack?'

Three months later I was pinching myself, appearing on *Top Of The Pops* introduced by Tony Blackburn and David Hamilton in week three as the record reached number seven in the UK charts. (Tony had chosen the song as his 'Record of the Week' on his Radio 1 breakfast show.)

'Simon May or may not!' said Tony cheesily, as I sat by the *TOTP* grand piano surrounded by lights and roving cameras, vowing never to forget this special moment.

A week before going to the BBC Studios to record my first *Top Of The Pops*, I received a letter from the legendary producer Johhny Franz, who was responsible for recording all the 1970s hits by Dusty Springfield, the Walker Brothers and many others. This was the second of two letters from him, the first written to me over ten years earlier. I will always treasure them both and when I want to inspire a young ambitious songwriter or singer today, I show them what Johnny wrote to me in 1965 and then in 1976.

I don't need to say anything more: his words say it all!

PHILIPS

PHILIPS RECORDS LIMITED

STANHOPE HOUSE · STANHOPE PLACE
LONDON W. 2.
PHONE · AMBASSADOR 7788
TELEGRAMS · PHILRECORD PHONE LONDON
CABLES · PHILRECORD LONDON

3rd September, 1965.

Mr. Simon May,
South Royd,
Station Hill,
<u>Devizes</u>.

Dear Mr. May,

Many thanks for sending your tape of "WHERE DID
YOU GET THAT LOVE". I have listened to this and whilst I feel
it shows that you have great talent in writing this type of material –
and also performing it for that matter – I do feel the song is not,
for want of a better word "direct" enough to become a hit and I
therefore regret I cannot make use of it.

I am extremely sorry about this and would like
to point out that each year I receive literally hundreds of tapes
from amateur writers but none of these show as much promise as you
do and I can only advise you to keep writing and letting me hear
your efforts for I feel sure that eventually you will achieve
success in this direction.

Yours sincerely,
PHILIPS RECORDS LIMITED

John Franz,
Artists and Recording Manager

DIRECTORS : J. W. A. LANGENBERG (DUTCH)   J. P. ENGELS (DUTCH)   L. GOULD

phonogram

PHONOGRAM LIMITED

Mr Simon May
c/o ATV Music Ltd
12 Bruton Street
London W1

LONDON W2 2HH

Stanhope House — Stanhope Place
Telephone: 01-262 7788
Telegrams: Phonrec London W2
Cables: Phonrec London W2
Telex: 261 583

Registered in England
Company No. 586873
Registered office address
Stanhope House — Stanhope Place
London W2 2HH

14th October 1976

PRIVATE & CONFIDENTIAL

Dear Simon

A brief note to tell you that I have just returned
from a short holiday and seen the charts.   I just
want you to know that I am as happy as you must be
with your great success.

Hope to see you soon.

Best wishes.

Yours sincerely

JOHN FRANZ
ARTISTE & REPERTOIRE MANAGER

'If You Leave Me Now' by Chicago was the competition to 'Summer of My Life', and due to my rather naïve and average performances on *TOTP*, Noel Edmonds' *Swap Shop* and all the other TV shows at that time, I stuck at Number 7 while Chicago raced to the Number 1 spot.

But I had made my mark. 'Summer of My Life' was a big hit and its success enabled me to plan my future life with Rosie.

Before I proposed, I joined her on my first trip to the North East where I met her dear mother Ann, sisters Sue and Jane and friends. Rosie's father Kit had died at a young age when she was fourteen. He fought in the 4th/7th Royal Dragoon Guards in a Sherman tank in Northern France. On D-Day afternoon he was at the sharp leading edge of the push into France from the beaches and suffered severe injuries before being hospitalized in England. Later, after the war ended, he died as a result of those injuries and sadly I never had the opportunity of meeting him and getting to know him.

Meeting all of the family and friends in Sunderland was like running a Geordie gauntlet. Who was this 'flash' pop star from the South who was dating their Rosie? I would like to think that my love of people, which knows no demographic boundaries, won through eventually. Geordies have no truck with pretension – they tell you how it is – and my West Country roots empathized with that culture very strongly.

Rosie's grandmother welcomed me with open arms: 'Simon, look after her,' she once said to me with tears in her eyes.

Rosie's older sister Sue lives with husband Kendall and their two children Zoë and Charlie in Gosforth, Newcastle upon Tyne. I have always enjoyed a special relationship with the city and our son Freddie remains a loyal supporter of NUFC to this day.

My other sister-in-law Jane lives with Don near to our Surrey home, so currently we get to see them and their two children, Pippa and Kit, a little more often... unlike my brother Michael and his wife Sandra who live somewhat further away in Wiltshire (with my nephew Alex) and my lovely niece Rachel and family.

My other nephew Matt and his wife Rute live in Portugal, and although all the May family do try to meet up every year at Christmas and keep in touch via telephone we don't get to see each other as much as Rosie's side of the family...

But as I said earlier, I'm in danger of fast-forwarding the story of my life!

OUR WEDDING in Wiltshire in the church of Market Lavington on 13th May 1978 was a lavish affair. Outside the church there was a long line of local friends and well wishers, and the local newspapers proclaimed on the front page: 'Local pop star comes home to wed!'

In 1979 Rosie and I bought a lovely cottage in the village of East Horsley near Guildford for a song – literally. We owe this to one of my co-produced hits which earned a lot of money, although I still believe that my colleague and main producer at the time never paid me every single pound of the royalties due to me. In 2008 when I met him again after all those years, he bounced up to me to renew our friendship and I have to say that I found it difficult to reciprocate. 'What goes round…'

(I believe in karma and in my next life I would like to come back as a Buddhist!)

Due to her special talent for organisation, Rosie was promoted to Head of Administration at ATV Music. Part of her job was purchasing drinks for the directors and champagne for the whole office whenever the Company enjoyed a new hit song in the Top Ten. ATV Music in the seventies was legendary and many of its young staff went on to hold high positions in the UK music industry. I have remained good friends with some of them, like Rob Sawyer and Stuart Slater, with whom I enjoy occasional lunches to reminisce about the good times, catch up on news of our ATV friends and chat about how our own families and careers are progressing.

Our A&R manager at the time was the legendary Eric Hall, who has since left the music industry to become one of football's most successful agents. Eric's expenses were eye-watering, but he earned his money. His catch phrase was 'Monster, monster' which he applied to any song, record or artist he was promoting.

I remember him telling us one day that he was going to lunch with Freddie Mercury. 'What, not *the* Freddie Mercury?' I asked. 'I only deal with *"The's"*,' was his quick reply.

In the year that 'Summer Of My Life' was enjoying its chart success in the UK, it also charted in several other European territories, including Germany (with my German version 'Sommerwein').

Engelbert Humperdinck also recorded his own version of the song. During my career as a writer I have pride in knowing that many other major artists like Frankie Valli, Sir Cliff Richard, Ruby Turner, Amii Stewart, Marti Webb, The Shadows and others have recorded my songs.

It was a hectic year of flying abroad to promote the record on TV shows in Europe. When 'Summer of My Life' reached Number 1 in the charts in Malta, Pye Records arranged for me to fly out on a promotional visit and perform at the President's Ball. Rosie was able to join me on this trip and we both enjoyed the lavish hospitality given to us by the President's Scottish wife and the Maltese Broadcasting Authority. We stayed at the best hotel on the southern tip of the island and when I was not rehearsing for the concert or engaged in personal appearances, we were chauffeured round the island and got the full VIP treatment.

The only downside to this was that I experienced a negative aspect of what it must be like to be a famous pop star (which at the time I seemed to be on the island, as I was top of their charts). From our early morning cup of tea in the hotel bedroom suite accompanied by requests for autographs and photo shots of myself with a beaming chambermaid, to the last point of our day, there was never a moment of privacy given to us.

At first it was a 'buzzy' novelty but it very soon became rather wearying. I can understand why some stars and celebrities are occasionally rude to those of their fans who have no inhibitions about 'going over the line' and inter-rupting private conversations in restaurants, on beaches, in hotel corridors or wherever.

I have the greatest respect for Sir Cliff who manages to get the balance absolutely right between giving time to his admirers but drawing a line where he tactfully with-draws from their intrusive demands. I love the story of one of his fans stopping him in the drive of his Weybridge home and after getting his autograph telling him that she had been told by God that she was the one whom Cliff would marry one day.

'That's strange,' replied Cliff, ''cos God didn't tell me!' And he gently but very firmly showed her out of the driveway before the iron gates closed.

Before performing to an audience of thousands at the President's Palace on an earlier evening, I gave a more intimate performance in the Dragonara Club overlooking the sea.

I was aware that as I was singing an up-tempo number, there was an elderly man at the back of the audience 'bopping away' and evidently enjoying my performance. After my spot was finished, Rosie and I walked past his table and a young lady sitting next to him introduced herself as the gentleman's nurse and carer.

'This is "Bomber" Harris,' she said proudly.

There was an instant role reversal as I felt privileged to be meeting one of our greatest British pilots and RAF

Air Marshal who had made a significant contribution to the victory of the Allied Forces in the Second World War.

Somewhere in my book collection, I still have a signed copy of Bomber Harris' biography with a little note saying: 'Really enjoyed your performance in Malta, Simon.'

Four or five tiring days of promotion and thousands of autographs later, it was time to leave Malta and return to the UK. The President's limousine duly arrived at our Hotel in Valletta and drove us to the airport. Customs formalities were waived and we were driven through security onto the tarmac where the President's secretary unloaded our cases and then accompanied us up the steps of the British Airways plane before bidding us farewell.

The pilot's cabin door was open and the President's secretary introduced himself to the chief pilot, then said, 'And these are your special guests for this flight, Captain: Simon May and his wife…'

'Simon who?' asked the pilot, which rather deflated the occasion and the high esteem which the people of Malta had shown me over the past five days.

In 1977, my follow up single 'Closest Thing to Heaven' flopped and my third release on Pye Records only crept into the Top 50. I remember a return visit to the *Top of the Pops* studio dressed in a kitsch white suit with a red rose and bottle of champagne on the grand piano, singing Ivor Novello's 'We'll Gather Lilacs', with a middle eight borrowed from Paul McCartney's 'All My Loving'. I am told that I *looked* great, but unfortunately the Musicians'

43

Union were in dispute with the BBC that week and insisted on performers singing live, as opposed to miming.

Even my mother couldn't bring herself to phone me the next day – I was so bad (in the old-fashioned sense of the word!). Either the orchestra was playing a semi-tone sharper than me or I was singing a semi-tone flat!

I think I must be the first artist to appear on *TOTP* and then drop out of the charts the following week, though this was something that became more common in later years.

But the experience of being vulnerable and failing by singing live was something I learnt from and which we avoided years later when I co-produced a new version of 'Knock On Wood', performed by Amii Stewart. The legendary Mike Mansfield directed an awesome pop video, which was well ahead of its time. No live vocals on that video!

'Knock On Wood' was a complete 'turkey' when first released in the UK. No airplay... no sales... nothing! However, it then reached platinum and Number 1 in the USA in 1979, selling over two million copies. On its re-release in the UK, it became a Top Ten hit. Confirmation of my credo that NO is spelt YES!

AFTER ROSIE and I had renovated our cottage, we very soon started a family. First, dear Lucy in 1980 who, after getting her degree at Newcastle University, was drawn to the music industry. She worked for EMI Music, then an artist management company and until 2015 for the music video hosting service Vevo. She married Nick in 2011 and gave birth to our first grandchild, Chloe Rose, in August 2014.

Rosie set about making our first real home warm and inviting for all our family and friends in East Horsley to visit. I feel so glad that my mother and father and Rosie's mother spent many happy times there with us.

Dear Olivia followed just over two years later and she and Lucy brought so much joy and happiness to our lives. So did Daisy and Freddie, who were to follow after a seven-year gap… but let's stay in the eighties for the moment.

In 1983 whilst we were still living in our lovely cottage, I decided to re-record my musical *Smike*. The BBC vinyl album starring Beryl Reid and Leonard Whiting had been deleted, so I embarked on an ambitious project in which we recruited about thirty of the best young singers we could find from all over UK who came from schools that had successfully mounted their own productions of *Smike*.

The 'Kids from Dotheboys Hall' descended on our Surrey home for a week. Ian Hughes created a stunning new orchestration of the show, which we rehearsed with the young actors at Parkside School in Surrey and recorded in my favourite Wimbledon Studio.

Jill Gascoigne, Oliver Tobias and Mike Holoway (the former heart throb member of the pop group Flintlock) sang the lead parts. And a talented youngster, Matthew

Paddon, gave a poignant and powerful performance as Smike.

We advertised the new cast album on Channel 4, but it was not effectively marketed either professionally or realistically. We lost a small fortune, but the recording was digitally remastered recently and still features on the *Smike* website. Without this new recording, which doesn't seem to have dated and which is used by many new producers of the show (including the backing tracks), I don't believe that *Smike* would still be enjoying its current success. Financially you could say that it was an unwise investment, but I don't regret it, because it was so enjoyable and in the long term has continued to give life to one of my most valued and loved musical works.

Anyone Can Fall in Love

WHEN 'SUMMER OF My Life' was in the charts in 1976, I got to know Leslie Osborne who worked for ATV Music in one of the back rooms of the company buildings. His main job was to get live performances of the publisher's hit catalogue on BBC Radio shows like *Friday Night Is Music Night*.

I like working with people of every age group. Whilst the other writers might have dismissed this eighty year old man as irrelevant, Leslie and I got on very well after my publisher Peter Phillips introduced us to each other, and before long Leslie had managed to persuade Ronnie Hazlehurst and other leading BBC conductors to re-arrange 'Summer of My Life' for live performances on Radio 2.

One day in 1982, Leslie called me into his office. 'Listen old boy, I would like you to meet Gerry Glaister, who is a good friend of mine and a top BBC TV drama producer.'

Gerry had produced a string of hit drama shows such as *Colditz* and *The Brothers* and was about to launch a new thriller series starring the veteran actor Michael Denison, called *Skorpion*.

I met Gerry and wrote the theme for *Skorpion*; a year later, after the success of the TV series, Gerry invited me to write not only the theme but the incidental (background) music to a new series starring Michael Denison, called *Cold Warrior*.

I had never 'written music to picture' before, and in those days the music was recorded 'live' to picture at BBC Lime Grove Studios just off Shepherds Bush. Conducting even a small group of musicians whilst the scene was shown on a large screen was extremely challenging, but because I knew the musicians I arranged to have unofficial 'pre-rehearsals' with them at home before the recording and managed to bluff my way through those sessions.

A few years later Peter Phillips took me to dinner with the great movie composer Jerry Goldsmith at his home in the Hollywood hills. The next day, I had the thrill of accompanying Jerry to the film studio where he had a massive orchestra to record his latest score to picture. As he conducted, he made each beat and nuance of his music work in synchronization with the pictures – something far more impressive than my first live session with five musicians at the BBC Lime Grove Studios, recording the music for *Cold Warrior*! And also much harder to accomplish without the benefits of modern technology that enables us to sync music to picture at twenty four frames per second (although without the assistance of a skilled programmer I find coping with the music software to achieve the same task just as challenging!).

The script editor on both of the Michael Denison series was a lovely guy called Tony Holland. Thankfully he was impressed with my skills as a composer and through Leslie got in touch with me in early 1984.

'Simon, Julia Smith and I are developing a new Soap for the Beeb called *E8* and we would like to meet you.'

I went to BBC Television Centre to meet Tony and the redoubtable Julia Smith.

Julia had directed early episodes of *Z Cars* and *Doctor Who* in the 1960s, and in the '70s worked with Tony as producer on the BBC's long-running hospital drama *Angels*. Her reputation as a formidable and much respected creative force filled me with trepidation as I entered the office. But her warmth and friendliness totally belied what I had previously heard about her. From minute one we hit it off. I was no threat to her talent and expertise. I was potentially the music department, and she and Tony needed a catchy theme to 'get the viewers out of the garden' to watch their new creation.

They showed me a model set of Albert Square created by the amazing set designer Keith Harris. I looked at photos plastered on the office walls of the actors who were on the shortlist to play all the characters in the Beale family, and the husband and wife landlords of the Old Vic... and they spoke excitedly about the eclectic mix of characters who would play their roles in this new soap opera based in the East End of London.

Later on, I learned that some of the leading actors would be changed. Anita Dobson, who played Angie, was a last-minute decision and probably the actress who was originally to have taken the part might to this day ruefully compare herself to Stuart Sutcliffe, the 'fifth Beatle who never was' and who failed at the last hurdle.

I scribbled notes of everything they said, as I always do, and agreed to come back soon with a musical sketch for the title music.

Three days later, I was back at Television Centre with my portable Walkman and a demo of my first *EastEnders* theme.

They hated it. I could see this from the glazed expression in their eyes (something I have since got so used to when presenting 'work in progress' to my client producers and directors), and so I went back to the drawing board.

They didn't want something 'edgy' and dark like the *EastEnders* characters.

They wanted something universal, almost feelgood to contrast with Albert Square and its gritty tough storylines. They needed a magic hooky tune with multi-ethnic colours as well as something that encapsulated the warmth of the Cockney character.

When they heard my new demo with the whistle playing the last hook of *EastEnders*, I saw Julia smile and knew that I had got them.

They immediately sent the demo tape to their graphic designer Alan Jeapes who I had worked with before, when he created the titles to *Cold Warrior*. Alan's idea to use the iconic shape of the River Thames as the logo for *E8* was a stroke of inspired creativity.

I received a contract from the BBC two days later, which offered me the princely sum of about £100 as the commissioning fee. But the prize was a potential PRS

(Performing Rights Society) royalty every time the theme would be played in the future.

'Do you get paid every time *EastEnders* is played?' I am often asked. 'Yes, but not as much as if I received £1 for every time I am asked that question!' is my stock answer.

The other question I am often asked is how I conceived of the *EastEnders* theme...

It started with a sunny morning, a cup of coffee and a simple LinnDrum pattern and attractive chord sequence, constructed at 10 a.m. in my Surrey home studio. And my fingers wandering over the keyboard to create a melody, the first seven notes of the scale... bar 3, a simple descent... and bar 4, where a kind of triplet was followed by a random passing note that made the tune different and unexpected.

I can't remember exactly how it happened. But it was fulfilling my criteria: goose pimples, a surging feeling within my heart and yes – tears of joy at the realization that I had discovered something that struck a chord and moved me emotionally.

Of course I didn't know at the time that it would become so memorable and be part of the national psyche. That would only happen because of the success of the programme and other factors way out of my control.

Where did that tune come from? Did it pre-exist and I discovered it as a sculptor reveals the statue in the rock? (Hoagy Carmichael, who composed the American standard 'Stardust' said: 'I didn't write it. I found it!') Was the *EastEnders* theme something I had written in an earlier sketching? I think so, but I don't know for sure. Does a mother remember the moment of birth? Most probably because that's an incomparably more painful and important experience! I can't really remember how the *EastEnders* theme happened, but it was my baby and I will never cease to be proud of its creation.

A composer's job is to compose. And by 11.30 a.m. on that life-changing morning, I had nailed the theme!

The actual arrangement took much longer. Ian Hughes and my musicians worked with me to combine a contemporary pop track with instruments like sitar and steel drums that reflected the multi-ethnicity of Albert Square, as well as the Bow Bells of East London, a human sounding whistle and a string arrangement which gave the finishing touches to the orchestration.

Apart from my melodies that were later refined and improved, my middle section for *EastEnders* (which still gets played in the 'Omnibus' edition and certain key episodes) originally lasted for eight bars. Julia and Tony asked me to shorten the theme so those eight bars were then compressed into four. Less is often more and writing to a producer's brief can often be liberating rather than constraining. The melody of the original middle eight was rather laborious, but by halving the structure I think the melody became more direct and memorable.

When I compose and record an important theme tune I always create a long version, partly because it might one day be marketed as a commercial three-minute recording, and partly because it's easier to edit a short version from a long one rather than the other way round. In other words it is better to create a novelette from a long story rather than expand a novelette into something longer, which would run the risk of being 'padded' and laboured. (Rather like the end of this paragraph!)

Creating a long version also gives you the freedom to experiment and take more risks than if you are only creating a short thirty-second version.

So with *EastEnders*, I created a three-minute version starting with the opening statement which was to become the opening title music.

Then we went into a fun development section where the mood changed and the tune was played as an old fashioned cockney knees-up variation, similar to the Russ Conway/Winifred Atwell style that I had played all those years ago in my father's furniture warehouse.

I was comfortable with that idiom. In fact, when I was in my early years of teaching at Kingston Grammar School I used to earn £3 a night playing in pubs in and around London, especially the East End, so it felt right to be adopting this authentic Cockney style of playing. I was once playing in a 'dodgy' East End pub accompanying the regulars as they sang songs of their choice, when a burly customer asked me, 'Do you know "How to Get to Leopold Street"?'

'Mmm, I don't know that one,' I replied. 'Can you sing me the start of the chorus and I'll follow you.'

He nearly thumped me. All he wanted was to know how to get to Leopold Street.

To return to the *EastEnders* recording... from that middle section, how could we get back to the more contemporary end section which had a different feel to the Cockney section? I knew that there would have to be a dramatic drum fill to create a musical distraction and bring us back to the feel of the main piece. That fill (now referred to as the 'doof doof') was a rhythmic reflection of the last triplet 'hook' in the main melody. It was therefore compatible but also unexpected and acted as a delightful bridge between the two different musical styles.

When I was mixing the tracks, I asked the engineer Neil to solo the drum fill which was played on the electronic Simmons drum kit by the very talented drummer Graham Broad. When I offered it to Julia and Tony as the dramatic start of the end-titles they loved it. (It was only years later that the drum fill was added to the opening titles.)

That short drum fill has been the subject of much curiosity and comment over the years. Every actor who receives his new script apparently goes to the last page first to see whether he or she has got the final 'doof doof' line. Shane Richie once told me that he was one of the privileged few to be given the last spoken line in his first episode on the show.

When *EastEnders* was first broadcast in 1985 I can still remember the thrill of walking down the street or shopping in a supermarket, hearing people humming or whistling my tune. And it *was* my tune. Although Leslie Osborne managed to get a co-credit (and share of the royalty!) because he was responsible for getting the gig, he didn't write a single note. He never even came to the recording studio. I'm not the first and won't be the last to hand over all or some of a royalty share to other 'co-writers'. Percy Sledge always said that he allowed Calvin Lewis and Andrew Wright, band members of the Esquires, to take *all* the writing credits of 'When A Man Loves A Woman', which he claims he played a major part in writing, because they gave him the opportunity to 'sing his heart out'. If that's all true I think my gesture to Leslie pales into insignificance!

My career went up a few bars as a result of *EastEnders* and *Howards' Way*, which I 'co-wrote' with Leslie in the same year. I could possibly have insisted on retaining the copyright of *EastEnders* for myself, but if I had done so, I would probably have lost the *Howards' Way* commission. (I will explain why shortly.)

I always think it's important to remember that on the day you leave this world you are allowed to say 'If only I hadn't…' but *never* 'If only I had…'

A year after the launch of *EastEnders*, the theme was nominated as best TV Theme of the Year in the Ivor Novello Awards 1986. A great honour, as the 'Ivors' are regarded as the most prestigious music awards in the UK calendar and I was more than excited to receive the nomination. I had recorded Ivor Novello's 'We'll Gather Lilacs in the Spring' ten years earlier. No Ivors winner had ever recorded one of his songs. Could this be a first?

Everyone felt we had an excellent chance of winning due to the huge success of the programme and the favourable public reaction to the theme tune. My publishers ATV Music booked a table for us all, and Rosie and I arrived at the Grosvenor House Hotel in Park Lane to see that they had rather prematurely ordered champagne at our table to accompany our luncheon before the Awards ceremony.

Rather like the Oscars, the awards are announced with that fateful opening of an envelope revealing the winner's name. When it was the turn of our category our table was hushed, hands ill-advisedly poised to reach for the champagne glass, and as the envelope was opened... I can still hear a voice saying:

'And the Award for best TV theme goes to ... *Edge of Darkness* composed by Eric Clapton.'

Ouch! You feel you are falling down a black hole, you have a deep empty pain inside your stomach, and you are inconsolably sad. At the same time, however, you are doing your best to smile at everyone who is looking at you, and raise your glass sportingly to your winning adversary sitting a few tables away.

All of us at some time in our lives have to face disappointments, whether it is an exam failure, a job not offered, a failure to be selected for a sporting team, losing a race or competition, or rejection of any kind.

I have always loved the lines from Rudyard Kipling:

> 'If you can meet with Triumph and Disaster
> And treat those two impostors just the same...'

Career-wise, I guess I've experienced a 50/50 mix of the two, and I have always tried to turn a 'No' into a 'Yes'! It has never happened instantly. I occasionally go into a dark mood for two or three days. But rarely any longer.

Shortly after the Ivor Novello Awards lunch, Julia Smith and Tony Holland invited me to the Elstree Studios to discuss the commissioning of two new songs for a music storyline in *EastEnders*, which they wanted to fill the 'quiet' summer transmission period. They were considering a storyline in which the young cast members Sharon (Letitia Dean), Simon Wicks (Nick Berry), Kelvin (Paul Medford), Eddie (Simon Henderson) and Harry (Gareth Potter) decide to form a band called The Banned and compete in a local rock competition.

At the same time the unfortunate 'Lofty' was going to try unsuccessfully to win the heart of Michelle (Susan Tully). One of the songs performed by The Banned and sung by Simon Wicks would play alongside that love story. Lofty was a loser in love, and in everything else for that matter.

For this project I invited Bradley and Stewart James to write the songs with me. They had been part of the team working with me in 1985 on *Howards' Way*, and although I have often written solo (as in 'Summer Of My Life'), I felt that a collaboration for this challenging project would achieve a better result than if I was working on my own.

Like Lofty, I had suffered a very recent experience of the pain of losing. I remembered how I felt at the Ivor Novello Awards and suggested to Stewart and Brad that the title of our Simon Wicks ballad should be 'Every Loser Wins'.

Over recent years the word 'loser' has taken on a slightly different connotation: someone who is a 'no-hoper'. For me, at that time, a 'loser' was someone who was the opposite of a winner: the idea of turning defeat into victory, a 'No' into a 'Yes', had an appealing symmetry about it.

As well as performing our second song 'Something Outa Nothing' The Banned featured Simon Wicks singing 'Every Loser Wins'. He also played it solo on the Queen Victoria upright piano. I remembered how Jack Barton had featured my songs in the dramas of *Crossroads*, and Tony Holland was using more or less the same idea for *EastEnders* in 1986.

When 'Every Loser Wins' was featured on the programme, the single released by BBC Records leapt into the Charts and stayed in the Number 1 slot for several weeks, selling over a million copies.

A year later, we were back at the Grosvenor House Hotel for the Ivor Novello Awards Ceremony. The James Boys and I received the Ivor Novello statuette for the biggest selling UK single of the year. I often tell this story to my students when I am reminding them how to spell 'No' correctly.

ANITA DOBSON was one of the *EastEnders* cast who I had great fun working with when she sang the vocal version of *EastEnders* in 1986. Not only is she a consummate professional, but also a very warm and kind person. Many years later, she and her husband Brian May happened to meet our daughter Daisy at the Edinburgh Festival. The following day Daisy saw her perform in the play *Greek*, Steven Berkoff's version of *Oedipus*, and was blown away by her performance. They all shared the same train journey back from Edinburgh a few days later, and Brian gave Daisy a badge of his charity 'Save The Badgers' which she still wears on her favourite coat today!

Since the launch of the programme I had received hundreds of letters from the public saying that the tune should be turned into a song and even sometimes sending me their suggested ideas. Don Black who had just written the wonderful words for *Howards' Way* was my natural choice of lyricist. Although I consider myself a lyricist as well as a composer I felt that Don would do a far better job, which indeed he did.

I am not sure how many people realize how original his lyric is – yes, it's easy to fall in love, but staying in love for a lifetime is much harder.

Always There

COMPOSING THE THEME and the music for *Howards' Way* was creatively one of the happiest periods of my career so far.

In the same year that I wrote *EastEnders*, Gerry Glaister invited me to meet him and invited me (and Leslie!) to write the music for a new series provisionally titled *Boatbuilders*, which he was developing for a new Sunday night series for BBC1.

It was all about the Thatcher years of wealth, creation and aspiration. A *Dallas* meets UK 'feelgood' drama set on the Solent estuary... and the story of the sea. How I loved the whole idea.

That was another of those very special mornings when I 'went with the flow' and was moved to compose a tune for a programme that was to reach the hearts of 17 million viewers on BBC TV on Sunday nights for the next six years.

Within what seemed like a matter of moments I had sketched the melody. A good tune should take roughly as much time to write as a listener has to hear and enjoy it. First thoughts. Passion. And that's what I did. The arrangement and production took several weeks, but learning to perform the basic melody took less than two hours.

For the main theme, I sampled seagull sounds to complement the intro 4 bars. Already you felt you were on the estuary smelling the sea and the distant ocean waves. After Gerry had accepted my offering of the main theme, I wrote different themes for the individual characters in the series, just as Wagner created different leitmotivs for all his leading players.

During the show's successful run I had the pleasure of meeting and getting to know Jan Harvey, Stephen Yardley and the other members of the cast, many of whom I have kept in touch with.

In year two of the series I invited Don to write lyrics to the tune which Marti Webb performed for the hit single 'Always There'.

⑨

My original lyric was 'Almost There' but Don knew better and turned it into a more positive and meaningful love song 'Always There', which of all my work became my mother's favourite composition.

Creating all the different themes for *Howards' Way* was done in the days before orchestrators could rely on the use of computer software. I would compose and perform a melody on piano and go through the manuscript arrangements with Ian Hughes. We would decide on the choice of instruments and Ian and I would discuss counterpart melodies, strings and other parts. Once the full orchestration was agreed and written into a master score, Ian would then copy the individual parts from the master score (like first violins, second violins, violas, cellos, oboe, flute and brass). The orchestra sections were recorded in separate sessions at RG Jones Studios before everything was mixed together. All of the strings parts (for the 'Main Theme', 'Abbey's Theme', 'Frere's Theme' and other variations) were rehearsed and recorded in two three-hour sessions. If we went over the three hours the Musicians Union overtime rates were quite costly, so time was of the essence.

I particularly remember the morning I arrived at the studio at 9 a.m. for the string session which I was to conduct at 10 a.m. sharp. The studio had been prepared the night before with microphones, music stands and chairs for ten violinists, four violas and four cellists. I wish I could say the same for the string parts. At 9.30 a.m. dear Ian was still sellotaping the violin pages together, which were strewn all over the studio reception floor!

However, the session began on time. I had got to know the string players from previous sessions and miraculously knew most of them by name. I relied heavily on Pat, the leader of the strings, who would interpret my emotions and musical nuances to all the players. I always introduced a session with top class musicians by explaining that I was Simon May not Simon Rattle, and that my conducting skills were limited. I would be able to conduct at the right tempo and give signals of crescendo and rallentando but would be relying on their skills and generosity to get the best result. I think the musicians preferred that honesty to any attempt to bluff total expertise which would have seemed arrogant. They were occasionally amused by my technical ignorance but I think they respected my compositional skills and passion to record my music as perfectly as possible.

'Guys,' I remember Pat saying once, 'I think Simon wants the first eight bars of section B played more *marcato*.' 'Yes can you give each note more attack and accentuation please,' I added. Pat whispered to me in as low voice as he could, 'That's what marcato means Simon!'

Writing the incidental music for the six series of *Howards' Way* was my real baptism of fire in the art of writing music to picture. Dave Hewson who is responsible for the ITV *News At Ten* theme composition and arrangement of Johnny Pearson's original theme graciously allowed me to work on the incidental music at his studio.

I'd like to think we were ahead of our time.

I took loads of (analogue) tapes of all my different themes to his studio, and Dave and I combined all of them with added new pieces into a blend of music that was seamlessly mixed to picture. Sometimes I played live to picture like the pianists in an old movie theatre, but more often than not, we used or edited the existing pieces which had already been recorded and mixed.

One music cue could combine as many as three or four different pre-recorded pieces dubbed onto one multi-track and joined by 'musical glue' to create a continuous piece for a sequence lasting over a minute. Today everything is digital and organized using computer software. But the fundamental rules don't change.

Dave is a very accomplished pianist but, as a former teacher, he insisted that I, not he, should be the one to perform all the joins and extra pieces needed to go with the pictures. I am grateful to him for my induction lessons in spontaneous composition and writing filmic music.

For several years, I would travel every week to the BBC Studios in Pebble Mill Birmingham to dub the twenty or so pieces for each episode. The deadlines were punishing. A courier would arrive at our home on Monday morning with the latest 50-minute episode. I would have to be at Pebble Mill Birmingham with all the final music cues by the Thursday or Friday.

Creating what is called 'incidental' music for TV drama is as different a job from writing TV themes as that of a solicitor and a barrister. Firstly the composer has to be briefed and agree with the director where incidental music is needed. This process is called 'spotting' and is an art in itself. The music must be discreet but enhancing, and start and finish at the most effective moment.

When I am composing incidental music as opposed to the main theme for a film or TV drama, I compare the function of the music to that of a chambermaid in a hotel I might be staying in. I would miss having my room tidied and the bed made up. It is a job that has to be done, but I wouldn't welcome the intrusion of the cleaner constantly clattering round my room whilst I am trying to read a newspaper or watch television. Incidental music must be exactly that: functional, not too obvious and not intrusive.

If you had music stopping and starting constantly in one long scene it would probably become very noticeable and irritating. If you are unaware of it, it is probably doing a very good job, and you would miss it if it wasn't there.

One later series of *Howards' Way* had such tight schedules that I remember working at Robin Black's Studio in Ripley for as long as forty-eight hours without even a fifteen-minute coffee break. Absolute insanity, and I simply could never take that punishing schedule again.

Robin was engineering on those sessions. He had worked earlier in his career for bands like Black Sabbath and Jethro Tull so was more used to the rock and roll stamina-draining lifefstyle than I was. He and his wife Judith, their late dear son William who is forever in our hearts, and daughter Rosanna have remained close 'family' friends since the time when all our young ones went to the same primary school in East Horsley.

YOU WON'T find any composer who doesn't re-state a favourite leitmotiv more than once in his repertoire, and one example in my case is 'Barracuda', the uptempo variation of the *Howards' Way* theme which was used from 1987 to 1990 (series three onwards) as the music for the closing credits. Connoisseurs of *Smike* will know that the development section of 'Barracuda' is a musical re-visitation of the instrumental development section in the musical's closing song 'Believe'. ㊱

Abbey and Frere were two of the main characters in *Howards' Way* and their themes are two of the many that I created for each character in the series. Apart from the main *Howards' Way* theme, they are probably my favourite leitmotivs of the score, although I also love the reflective ㊲ ㊳ version of *Howards' Way* and how it was used to establish the characters and atmosphere of the programme from the very opening episode of series one.

Howards' Way ran for a phenomenal six series and was compulsive and much loved viewing in the UK, Australia, New Zealand and other English speaking territories abroad.

The pain and deep sadness of losing my father and mother and Rosie's mother in the 1990s is much softened by the comfort of knowing that they lived to share with us the success and happiness of *Howards' Way*, *EastEnders* and not a few hit records.

Howards' Way took me to new situations. In series four, my father's sister Auntie Gwen introduced me to Simon Lockyer, her grandson and my second cousin fresh out of the Royal Academy of Music, who joined the team and became one of my regular talented collaborators – joined later by the equally talented John Brant.

Madness and Serendipity...

TOWARDS THE END of 1986, after an exciting year of success with *EastEnders* and *Howards' Way*, I composed the theme for the BBC *Holiday Programme* when it was presented by Cliff Michelmore and Jill Dando. The Head of Graphics whom I worked with was a gentle man called Max. Just like Alan Jeapes who designed the opening title sequence of *EastEnders*, he was a delight to work with. There was more time for enduring friendships in those earlier days. We worked hard of course, but the turnaround was more leisurely. Today you can't tell a client that your updated work is 'in the post'. They want it e-mailed or uploaded instantly.

The recording studio that I was using at the time was RG Jones in Wimbledon. Gerry Kitchingham was the senior engineer with whom I worked regularly.

Although recordings in 1986 were digital, we still used tape machines either on 32 tracks or 24 tracks to record all the different instruments. Not the same as today's music software which enables you to record as many separate tracks as you like.

My 'Holiday Suite' comprised four separate movements, all needing a large number of individual tracks to cater for a big orchestration. 32 tracks were not enough to record all of the instruments. So we linked up two

⑪

multi-track machines, giving us 56 separate tracks to work with. The four separate movements were at different tempos and with different instrumentation. We were in effect recording four complicated pieces of music on the same session.

To quote Rudyard Kipling once more: 'Everyone is more or less mad on one point.'

I think my workload was getting to me and the team. I came out of one session at 3.00 a.m. to find that my car had been totally wrapped in cling film by the boys on the session!

The maddest thing I can remember about recording music onto physical tape was many years ago at Audio Studios in London, when Greg Walsh the engineer was re-winding the tape of our final important mix, and in a moment of distraction omitted to press the stop button. This resulted in the tape having a mind of its own and spinning round and round uncontrollably before it all unwound off the tape spool. Our recording of the final master mix ended up in a massive heap on the studio floor like a pile of loose knotted knitting wool, and Greg had to spend the next three hours painstakingly re-assembling our precious master recording tape onto its spool without creasing or damaging it.

IN 1988, I was commissioned to compose the Seoul Olympic theme with top composer Richard Mitchell. The ITV Executive Producer was coincidentally Richard

68

Russell, a good friend whose family also lived in East Horsley and whose children went to the local school with our two eldest daughters.

Even more coincidentally, this was the year that the Great Britain Hockey Team won gold. When I taught at Kingston Grammar School until 1973, I coached hockey three afternoons a week and one of my Under 13 Eleven was Richard Dodds who went on to become the Captain of the GB Team in 1988. The Producers of the Olympic Programme played on this coincidence and invited me to the ITV Studios on the night that the GB Hockey Team won the Finals, and I had the pleasure of chatting to Richard via satellite. The writer of the Olympic theme congratulating one of his former pupils on winning gold on primetime TV is the kind of serendipity that you don't enjoy very often.

The hand of fate has helped me in many ways since I left teaching, and there are several ex-KGS pupils who have made it to senior positions in the TV and Radio industry. One of them, Rod Natkiel, was Head Boy at KGS and became Head of BBC Network at Pebble Mill Birmingham. He was kind enough to commission me to write the main theme for Pebble Mill *Morning Daytime* – a strange reversal of roles that he was now employing me and I was ironically calling him 'Sir'!

Tony Fish, another of my former pupils, worked for BBC Radio 1 and became Head of BBC Radio Newcastle. He always generously welcomed me when I was on a local radio tour to drop in for an interview at his station.

There are other ex-pupils who continued to play a part in my life after I stopped teaching at KGS. I try to keep in touch and occasionally meet up with some of them at reunions. And it was great to be asked to help the School with their new production of *Smike* in 2006, to coincide with the inauguration of the new Performing Arts Centre opened by Her Majesty the Queen.

I have been so fortunate to have worked with some of the greatest UK musicians and singers during my forty year long career: Peter Whitfield, Dave Goodes, Ant Clark, Dave Cooke, Graham Broad, Quentin Williams, Alan Murphy... the list is endless and I apologize if I have not mentioned you all by name, guys! But you know who you are and I hope PPL (Phonographic Performance Ltd) does too. As opposed to PRS, which collects writers' royalties, PPL collects and distributes royalties for musicians and singers who have performed on any significant recording which is broadcast here and overseas. Any young musician reading this, do make sure you become a member.

And whilst on this subject, any composer or lyricist at the start of their career should without question join BASCA (the British Academy of Songwriters, Composers and Authors). The benefits of helpful advice, seminars and networking opportunities which this great organization offers are enormous for any writer, whether established or not. At a time when the value of intellectual copyright is being threatened worldwide, the work they do to represent our interests is something no individual writer can achieve on their own, and for this reason alone BASCA deserves all of our support.

I AM often asked if Rosie is musical. A definite yes to that one. She is my second pair of ears and has an unerring ability to judge my compositions and songs better than any A&R department or TV producer. Once she and I even worked together on a song: 'People Like You', which she sang for the title music of a BBC documentary series called *People*, which was all about ordinary people doing interesting things. ⑭

This show was fronted by Derek Jameson, a former newspaper editor who became an unlikely but popular TV presenter, and produced by Peter (now Sir Peter) Bazalgette, affectionately known to his friends and colleagues as Baz. Baz would eventually leave the BBC to create *Big Brother* and *Deal or No Deal* for Endemol, but before that he and I worked together on a number of projects. After he commissioned me to write the new theme for the long-running BBC2 show *Food & Drink*, he and I became good collegiate friends and he later invited me to write the theme for *People*.

When I was writing the theme song, called 'People Like You', I was trying to think of a suitable girl to record the demo vocals. I happened to hear Rosie singing away in the kitchen at the time and I thought 'Look no further, she's the one!' Not only did Baz love the song, but he also wanted Rosie to perform it and to be featured in one of the show's programmes as the 'regular housewife' singing the title music of the programme.

On the strength of this, BBC Records decided to release a full length version of the song, to be performed by the artist known as 'Melody'!

The director of *People* was Jeremy Mills. Years later, Jeremy went on to form Lion TV and produce programmes like BBC TV's *Castaway*, for which Simon, John and I wrote the music.

On the day when the camera crew were arriving at our home in East Horsley to film the story of Melody singing the *People* theme song, I woke up and became aware of an unusual thumping sound in our bedroom. I feared that the gas boiler was on its last legs and then realized that the sound was actually next to me and was Rosie's heartbeat, pounding away in panic attack mode. She was understandably nervous and anxious about having to perform in front of the cameras!

It all went very well, actually, and the day was a happy one. Lucy and Olivia, at a very young age, got drawn into the filming and the BBC record of 'People Like You' reached a modest chart position the week after the programme featuring Melody was broadcast.

The best part for Rosie was going away with her mother for a couple of days break in Dorset after the programme had been shown on BBC TV and being approached by a family in the hotel car park. 'Our daughter thinks you are Melody,' said the father of the family. 'Can she have your autograph, please?'

'Melody' still dines out on that story.

More To Life

I N 1990, GERRY Glaister commissioned me to write
the theme for *Trainer*, the follow-up series to *Howards'
Way*, which ran for two seasons on BBC1. This was the
time when network producers were beginning to lose
autonomous control over their shows. Gerry's vision was
being dictated by higher executives who were unwilling
to take risks on one person's judgement. If you look at all
the big successes on the big and small screen over recent
years, you will find the vast majority were driven by one
passionate believer who worked with his or her close
team and wasn't creatively overridden by a committee
of 'suits' (however indispensable they may be in other
ways!).

The star of *Trainer* was a charismatic actor called Mark
Greenstreet whom I met a couple of times on the set and
kept in touch with when the series ended. Since then he
and I became and have remained close friends.

Although I consider myself to be a decent lyricist, I
have always enjoyed creative collaboration. Don Black's
lyrics to the *EastEnders* and *Howards' Way* themes had
worked well, so why not ask my good friend Mike Read
to write the lyrics for the main theme that I had written
for *Trainer*? This would become the song 'More to Life'. ⑮

I had first got to know Mike in the 1970s when he was a DJ at the local Thames Valley Radio Station 210. He and Steve Wright presented a great afternoon show aptly called 'Read and Wright', and I was a guest on their programme, having written a new ident jingle for the station.

Mike, Steve and I hit it off, and they were the first of many other DJs like Chris Evans, John Humphrys, Gloria Hunniford, John Dunn, Ray Moore, Peter Powell, Graham Dene, Peter Gordon and Breakfast Bev, Julian Clegg, Paul Owens, Christian O'Connell, Neil Rosser and so many others who have interviewed me and whose apparently effortless technique as interviewers has always been a source of admiration to me.

I also guested on Mike's morning show *Saturday Superstore* on BBC Children's TV in the early 1980s. Over the years we became good friends and still are.

Writing with Mike is an interesting experience. His great talent is unquestioned. I normally collaborate in a more structured and 'interactive' way. With Mike, writing 'More To Life' for a TV drama series about racing horses was more exciting than actually riding one of the wildest horses on the race course.

However I'm sure that if you asked him for his memories of our friendship he will counter with the story of me waking him at 6.30 a.m. and excitedly asking him if he would be kind enough to write the Preface to one of my forthcoming albums. We both enjoy each other's eccentricities in equal measure.

Mike's lyrics were fabulous. 'Who should we get to perform this?' we asked ourselves.

The next day, Mike was at his friend Cliff Richard's house in Weybridge selling him the idea of performing the end-titles song for the follow-up series to the highly successful *Howards' Way* series, and of notching up another success in the endless list of Cliff Richard hit records spanning over five decades.

Meeting and getting to know Sir Cliff Richard was one of the most thrilling and privileged events of my professional career. I had always been a fan, and can remember taking one of my first girlfriends to our local cinema to see *Summer Holiday*. I also won't forget seeing Cliff live at the London Palladium, exuding (as he still does) charisma and stardom.

Thankfully Cliff loved the song and two months later we had the enormous pleasure of going to RG Jones Studios in Wimbledon, which at that time was where most of my recording was done and which also happened to be Cliff's favourite studio.

After listening to the vocal mix of 'More To Life', newly arranged and produced by Paul Mossell, Cliff kindly invited us all to join him and his party for an Indian meal in Wimbledon.

And the friendship grew from there. Rosie stepped into Mike Read's shoes or rather ski boots to join Cliff and friends for a skiing holiday in Lech, Austria. Mike had to drop out at the last minute and my dear wife is never one to miss the chance of a holiday! Those happy skiing trips together were to continue for another fifteen years or so.

She and Cliff became very good friends during that first skiing trip. Princess Diana was skiing with her two children William and Harry during the same week, and they agreed to meet up with Cliff and his party for a musical evening. Sadly this was not to be, as Diana's holiday was cut short by the illness and swift death of her father Earl Spencer.

Until a few months later, when Charles Haswell, one of Cliff's close friends who had joined the skiing holiday, arranged a dinner party in his sumptuous home in Barnes to which we were invited to join Diana and ladies-in-waiting, and also her bodyguard Ken Wharfe and other friends for a reunion evening with Cliff. (I learned later that Ken can vocally mimic an acoustic bass guitar and actually sound far better than the real thing!)

The evening was a closely guarded secret. Our instructions were to be there half an hour ahead of the royal party. The etiquette of meeting Princess Diana was explained to us all: you must address her as Ma'am until she invited you to be less formal; you must wait until spoken to; and so on. When I was introduced all I could do was be overwhelmed by her stunning beauty and the knowledge that I was meeting an icon.

Rosie had no such inhibitions and proceeded to chat to Diana, enquiring about her children and swapping stories about the challenges of bringing up young ones.

After dinner Cliff and Mike Read played songs on their guitars, performing 'Summer Holiday', 'Travelling Light' and 'Move It'. I'm sure EMI would have loved to market a live album of 'Cliff Sings to Diana' but it never happened.

It would have been a best seller! In any case, Rosie and I were privileged to be part of a very special evening.

My next encounter with royalty was not until 2005 when Kingston Grammar School (founded by Queen Elizabeth I) celebrated the opening of their new performing Arts Centre and generously included two songs from *Smike* to perform to Her Majesty when she opened the Centre. A new production of *Smike* was to be the first artistic project in the Arts Centre in a month's time and this short extract was presented to the Queen as a taste of what KGS was producing that year.

I had the honour of being presented to Her Majesty before the performance. True to form, I was speechless at the moment of introduction!

What anyone who hasn't met and spoken to the Queen won't be aware of is that in her handbag which she always carries is a little *aide-mémoire*, written by her advisors. This briefs her on whoever she is meeting, and has a list of relevant questions that she might choose to ask. I'm not saying this always happens and the handbag is often closed, but I am convinced that Her Majesty does have little sneak previews just before her subjects are introduced to her. If I'm wrong then all I can say is that she is extremely well briefed beforehand and has an amazing memory. She asked me if I was enjoying the new KGS production of *Smike*, how did it feel to return to my school after all these years and how much had I enjoyed teaching there.

I would have loved to reciprocate and ask her a couple of questions but that is strictly against all protocol. And it's funny how your mind works on such a special occasion. There I was, talking to Her Majesty, surrounded by press, minders and VIPs and for a crazy moment, I remember imagining the possibility of behaving inappropriately and hitting the headlines the next day. But of course you don't go there. All normal people have inhibitive mechanisms in our brains which constrain us from doing stupid and dangerous things like jumping off a high bridge. But these thoughts do cross your mind for a brief second, don't they?

'More To Life' was a respectable hit record to add to Sir Cliff's Collection and entered the charts at Number 23. Not the huge hit we had hoped for, one of the main reasons being that EMI had their annual conference at the end of the week's record release, so the all important marketing of the single was, I have always believed, compromised. In those days if the record companies didn't regularly supply enough 'promotional' copies to the chart shops there wouldn't be enough 'ticks' to keep the single high in the charts.

However, Mike and I won the Television & Radio Award for best TV Theme with 'More To Life' in 1992, and for me this was a delightful rerun of receiving the TRIC Award for *Howards' Way* a few years earlier.

Sir Cliff spends less time in the UK than he used to back then, but we still enjoy his friendship and go to his concerts whenever we can. Rosie and I will always cherish the memory of being invited to join him and his eighty guests for his 60th birthday cruise in the Mediterannean.

This was one of the most amazing weeks of our lives. The guest list was an interesting mix of Cliff's showbiz and non-showbiz friends, including Mike, Olivia Newton- John, John Farrar, Sir Tim Rice, Bobby and Trudy Davro, Gloria Hunniford and husband Stephen, Brian Bennett and Bruce Welch of the Shads, Sue Barker and her husband, Helen Hobson (who starred in Cliff's musical *Heathcliff*), Cheryl Baker of Bucks Fizz, Graham and Julie Dene, Shirley Bassey (on Cliff's birthday night dinner), Alan Farthing, Bill Latham (who was managing Cliff at the time) and many others, not forgetting our mates Malcolm Reeves and Tony Ferrari whose idea it was to arrange the Birthday Cruise!

Without exception everyone got on so well with everyone else. There were no pretensions or demands from anyone. Each night the dinner table arrangements changed and afterwards we all assembled in the club bar where the Shads, Bobby Davro, Gloria Hunniford, Mike Read and of course Cliff entertained.

Even I was allowed a spot in which I played a couple of pieces, and also accompanied Sue Mappin (the Executive Director of the Tennis Foundation Charity until 2010), performing a rather challenged rendition of a song that I can't and won't try to remember! Sue's vocals bore striking similarities to my *TOTP* performance of 'We'll Gather Lilacs'!

There was a moving wedding ceremony on deck to tie the knot of two of the guests, and also a very poignant awareness that dear Jill Dando who had been cruelly murdered in April was not with us. She and Alan Farthing were to have married in September. This was the first occasion we shared with Alan following Jill's death.

I will always remember how kind she had been to me on an earlier encounter, telling me how she loved my music, when it was actually me who was her greatest fan and admirer.

I also won't forget Rosie and me playing tennis doubles with Olivia Newton-John, Mike Read and other guests when the cruise party stopped off at one of the smartest hotels in Majorca – which was a bit special and something to brag about to your grandchildren one day!

We were sharing a 60th birthday party celebration with one of the nicest men in show business. And yes, in answer to the question that everyone always asks me, you get with Cliff what you see. No hidden agenda. He is genuinely a sincere and good person.

But if fans do abuse his niceness, he is capable of sticking up for himself. I heard that after the week's cruise when Cliff extended his holiday (this was his hard-earned sabbatical year!), he went back to the ship as a VIP guest for a holiday in the Caribbean. He was apparently approached on deck by a rather loud and intrusive guest who went way over the 'permitted' time for autographs and chat. After monopolising Cliff for quite a while the gentleman said to Cliff: 'Well, this is going to be a great cruise. We'll try not to get in your way too much.'

'I'm counting on that promise,' is what I'm told Cliff replied!

Eldorado

IN 1991, JULIA Smith and Tony Holland were developing their follow up TV soap to *EastEnders* with Executive Producer Verity Lambert. Set on location in Spain, this was to be the Euro hit drama series about the lives of expats from Britain settling in the Spanish sunshine village of Eldorado.

The concept was brilliant. I was flattered and excited when Julia and Tony invited me to a meeting in London to discuss composing the theme for the show.

A couple of years earlier, I had written a musical called *Mefisto* based on Goethe's *Faust* which, alas, never came to anything. It was backed by a city financier Ken Renton who invested in the project with money diverted from investment funds and which Ken's company looked after.

Ken was a charismatic guy and passionate about funding the arts. Unfortunately, all of the investors who lost their money in his company and the City of London police might not agree with my description of Ken. He was jailed for embezzlement and misappropriation of funds shortly after the *Mefisto* project ended.

I really liked Ken and couldn't believe it when I heard of his arrest. I sent a supportive letter addressed to him in Ford prison via his wife but never received a reply, and I often wonder what happened to them both.

But I am digressing…

⑯ There was a song in *Mefisto* that I loved called 'When You Go Away'. It was sung by Gretchen, the lead girl in the story, who was made pregnant by Faust and then deserted by him as he went on a wild life spree. The message of her song was a simple plea of love: *When you go away on your journey, I want to come with you and not be left without you.*

Their relationship was doomed from the start. *'It was over before it had begun'* was my opening line of the first verse. I never realized until later that the lyric would have a deep irony in the vocal version of *Eldorado*, and something that the press picked up on. *Eldorado* was doomed to be a failure from the start.

Before all the tears and recriminations of the series a year later, we all believed that the show would be a hit sequel to *EastEnders*. My instincts told me that a re-working of the song from *Mefisto* would make an excellent theme for the title music. The strong ascending melody going up the scale in a completely different way to the *EastEnders* theme was crying out for a Spanish guitar.

When I played the re-worked demo instrumental to Julia, Tony and Verity I put my cards on the table and told them that the tune already existed in my musical of Faust but that I had re-arranged it with a Spanish feel for the programme. Just as well that I did, because some kind soul wrote to Julia after the first episode was transmitted to tell her that the theme was a steal from one of my old musicals. 'I know,' Julia replied to the fan. 'Simon told us.'

I sometimes quote this story to my students when encouraging them always to be honest in their career. I explain that among other things it's easier to remember the truth rather than try to make up consistent stories that are based on lies.

In the recording of the theme music I employed four different acoustic guitarists to play the chords and melody of the theme. We mixed the four performances together which resulted in a rich blend, something that one guitar performance would have never created.

When we were mixing the final master, Julia was quite difficult and demanding. She was getting confused and irritated with all the different guitar tracks that I was offering.

And then in a conversation that I will always remember, she took me aside and said, 'Simon, a lot of people who work for me might say I'm daunting and rather bossy.'

'Not me,' I replied, smiling. 'You have always been very kind and honest with me.'

She gave me a big hug.

She was one of the best and most generous producers I have ever worked for.

Sadly, there were initial fault lines in the production values and early scheduling of *Eldorado*. Not all the actors were experienced Equity players, and more time and experimentation would have enabled them to use their talent better. The casting was fine but the expectations of the schedulers did not allow the baby to grow into the smash hit series that it deserved to become. The first episode was 'rushed out' to meet scheduling deadlines and the critics had a field day.

Alan Yentob, the new controller of BBC1, gave the producers what I believe was an unrealistic task of turning the show round within six months. Julia was fired and the new producers Corinne Hollingworth and Verity Lambert made valiant and praiseworthy efforts to get the show on track. Although the ratings and production values improved in that short space of time, the programme was still axed at the end of a one-year run. Faith and belief in new programmes in this new era of broadcasting were like ice in the sun – short-lived and too impatient for instant success.

After about four months of *Eldorado* hitting the UK TV screens, Rosie and I flew to Spain to spend time with Julia on the set and we had dinner with her in Mijas on the same day that she was fired. I knew something was wrong from the moment she greeted us. During our dinner in the mountain village overlooking the Med she confided the bad news to us with tears in her eyes.

I remember watching one of the last lunchtime transmissions of *Eldorado* and our son Freddie, who was only four years old, turned to me and said: 'Daddy, we won't be hearing your music again, will we?'

When *Eldorado* was coming to the end of its run, the vocal version of *Eldorado* 'When You Go Away', performed by my lifelong friend Johnny Griggs, was released as a single and was strongly supported by the 'Save *Eldorado*' fans. The opening prophetic line of the song, 'It was over before it had begun', still haunts me today.

Julia and Tony were two of the great innovators of British television drama and I have enormous respect for the BBC Drama Department who after Julia's death (but still in Tony's lifetime), created a special credit for them as creators of *EastEnders*. That credit remains on screen today.

I am still proud of the instrumental and vocal versions of *Eldorado* and will always remember the cast, production team and fans with great affection. Who knows, an enterprising producer might one day re-visit the format and create the hit soap that I believe it deserved to be.

Sturm und Drang…
into Peaceful Waters.

I T IS A truism to say that we all make mistakes. I have never known anyone who has not. I am no exception. Actually I have probably made more mistakes than most people but possibly balanced this with some very good calls that have resulted in an unusual and successful career. My personal 'yin & yang' has brought me Number 1 hits in the USA and the UK… and near bankruptcy.

In recent years I've calmed down and don't sail as close to the wind as I used to. However in my younger days and early middle age I have to admit to a large degree of vanity and arrogance which had bad consequences.

One morning in 1993, I decided to produce and finance a national tour of the UK with the Simon May Orchestra. I promised Rosie that although it had elements of risk, the tour would not jeopardise our home and lifestyle. How wrong I was. At that stage of my life I hadn't learnt the true difference between self-belief and self-delusion. To cut a long and rather painful story short, I contracted two soloists Mark Rattray and Emma Robbins (sister of Kate), for a month's tour, and arranged for hundreds of young singers from 'Smike schools' in the UK to perform in one of the concerts to be held in their local area. I booked fifteen

Above: My parents at my wedding to Rosie, 1978.

Below left: With my brother Michael. (I'm on the left!)

Below right: Pre-teen me!

I

Above: Hazy memories of my first group, The Dominant Sect.
Below: Simon Plug & Grimes.

Above: Stephanie de Sykes & Rain in rehearsal in Wiltshire with fake cotton reel microphones.

Below: Stephanie de Sykes & Rain performing at the Savoy Hotel in 1974.

Above left: Rosie likes this shot of me taken during the Summer of My Life, 1976.

Above right: On page 7 of the Sun in the '70s!

Below: Posing for PR shots in Malta, 1976.

Inset: Rosie and me in Corfu, 1977.

Above: Our wedding day, May 1978.

Above: ATV Music Convention in Marbella in the mid-1970s. A demure Jackie Gill front right, Eric Hall in very front, and a younger me in the back row. (Nostalgia fans: can you spot Tony Hiller and the Brotherhood of Man, one of the New Seekers and Kenny Lynch?)

Below: Lucy's Christening Day.

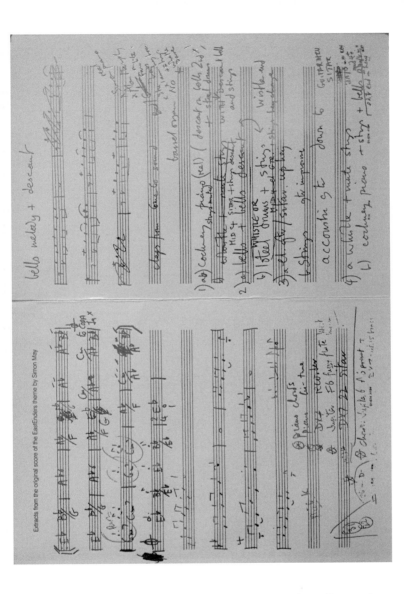

Above: My early sketched notes of E8 which the EastEnders office used as the front of one of their Xmas cards!

Next pages: EastEnders cast and production team in 1985.

Above: Sheet music cover for the *Howards' Way* theme, showing the Howard family: Leo (Edward Highmore), Jan (Jan Harvey), Tom (Maurice Colbourne), Lynne (Tracey Childs).

Above left: Me and my first Macintosh mini computer the year I wrote
EastEnders!

Above right: 19 Simon and Melody in duet!

Below: The May family in our new home at the start of the new century!

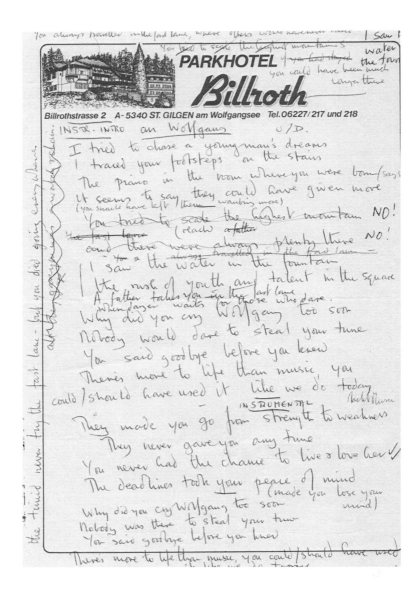

Above: Lyrics for my song 'Wolfgang' scribbled on hotel stationery.

Above: Rosie ski-ing with Sir Cliff in Austria!
Below: The May family at Olivia's wedding.

Above: The Boys at John's wedding. From left to right Chue (RG Jones Studio manager), Ant Clark, Simon Lockyer, Keith Bessey, John, me and Ben Robbins.

Below: The May Family in July 2015 with granddaughter Chloe!

Above: 'Bobby Beale' (Eliot Carrington) and me at the *EastEnders* 30th Anniversary.

Above: Rosie and me in Thailand, 2015.

musicians, a production crew, hire and transportation of all the equipment and thirteen prestigious venues including Drury Lane, the Royal Concert Hall Nottingham and the Fairfield Hall Croydon.

Ticket sales in many of the venues didn't come anywhere near to matching my cost projections. We even had to cut our losses and cancel two concerts where advance sales were dreadful. We lost an eye-watering amount of money and had to sell our lovely cottage in East Horsley and rent a new home in the village.

However, all the venues, artists, musicians and technicians were paid. I didn't organise the structure of the tour project in such a way that I could hide behind bankruptcy. Rosie and I and our children were the only substantial losers, although there was one (and only one) teacher who never forgave me for pulling the concert in Manchester that her kids were going to perform in. I offered to go to her school and put on a special performance for her parents and pupils, but she would have none of it. Her understanding that my family and I were suffering a major setback and about to lose our home was limited.

After the concert tour fiasco it took me a long time to learn fully the lessons of a major error of judgment and help us claw our way back to security and true happiness.

Before moving on, I wouldn't like you to think that it was all an unmitigated disaster. Yes, it was financially a life-changing failure, but artistically and from the reactions I received from our audiences it was a success. The music and the songs were performed to a very high standard, and as for the thousand or so youngsters who sang songs from *Smike*, they sang their hearts out at every concert, whilst the Orchestra, Mark and Emma performed my favourite themes and hit songs. BBC TV also featured the tour and my career in a special Pebble Mill documentary. As well as that, the hard learned lessons of budget planning and control have stayed with me ever since.

Do I regret that it all happened? I regret *how* it happened but the whole experience was invaluable and something to be proud of. In hindsight, unquestionably, I should have hired one large London venue to celebrate my music for one special evening and not attempted a major national tour. Have I learned more from my failures than my successes? Yes… but how many people can say they performed solo at Drury Lane with a fifteen-piece orchestra and a choir of two hundred, and likewise at ten of the most prestigious concert halls in the UK?

I won't ever have to ask myself the question: 'I wonder what would have happened if…'

AFTERWARDS, THE real start of the fight-back came in 1995 when Ray Thompson, Executive Producer of Cloud 9/Sanctuary, whom I had got to know during the *Howards' Way* project, invited me to be his composer for an exciting film/TV project, *The Enid Blyton Adventure Series*. Olav Wyper, my manager at the time, negotiated an excellent deal with the film company. As well as receiving generous commissioning fees for composing and recording all the music in the UK, I was also to be well paid for assisting the inexperienced post-production team in Wellington, New Zealand to put all of my music together and make it fit to picture, just as we had done ten years earlier when creating all the 'incidental' music for *Howards' Way*.

'I'll Always Stand By You', which I wrote as the theme song for the title music of the series, sums up the resilience, love and loyalty which Rosie showed throughout this whole stormy period of our lives. Although the lyric is about the friendship between the four youngsters in the Enid Blyton storyline, it is also as much about Rosie and her courage as anything else. As with other lyrics I have written, I love the words to connect with more than one situation. I believe it helps to give them a more universal appeal.

Flying first class to New Zealand and staying in one of the nicest hotels in Wellington was a luxury. Every morning I would walk from the hotel to the post-production studios in Wellington, and occasionally drive along the lakeside motorway to the Cloud 9 offices in Upper Hut, a few miles miles away from the city, for meetings with Ray Thompson and his production team. On a clear blue sky day this was an exhilarating experience. On a windy Wellington day it was not quite so special.

In the first of seven series when I worked in New Zealand, I was away from home for about five weeks. In later series, as the post-production team learned the ropes of music editing, the trips got much shorter because my experience was not so needed.

Turning left into first class as I embarked on the Air New Zealand plane was a treat and obviously much more pleasant than flying tourist class, although on one occasion my arrival at the departure desk wasn't quite as carefree as one might have wished.

Rosie had dropped me off at the first class departure point at Heathrow Terminal 3 and I was now about to board the Air New Zealand flight. 'Mr May?' enquired the airline official as I presented my passport and boarding card in the departure lounge.

'Yes…' I replied.

'You've got your wife's car keys!'

Oops. Rosie, I learnt later, had returned to her car to pick up Daisy and Freddie at school, and realized that after parking the car in the short term car park, I had pocketed the car keys. She had rushed back to the terminal and pleaded with the airline supervisor to contact me before I boarded – a rather embarrassing task for her because she had just harangued the same supervisor an hour earlier for check-in misdemeanours!

However, she got the car keys back and managed to complete the school run just in time.

Like my twenty-five hour first class flight to New Zealand, my first week in the St James luxury hotel in Wellington was also very enjoyable. However, after the first two weeks those long lonely weekends got to me and I missed everyone at home desperately.

I do however have fond memories of one particular long weekend when I took off on my own and drove down South Island, taking in the stunning views of the expansive scenery of mountains and lakes. The Kiwis are a very friendly and hospitable people who still have strong ties and affection for the Brits, and if any of you are planning a trip to Asia or Australasia, I thoroughly recommend that you try to include South Island as a 'must' in your itinerary.

I did also have the chance to spend a few days in Sydney, which my employers generously treated me to, after an exceptionally long and debilitating series of re-routed flights to Wellington lasting over forty-five hours. I particularly enjoyed walking along the beaches just outside Sydney, including Bondi Beach, which is one of the favourite locations for many of the Aussie movies and soaps that I enjoy watching. (By the way, my two favourite soaps happen to be *EastEnders* and *Home & Away*!)

The Enid Blyton 'Adventure' series was shown in over one hundred and thirty countries around the world, and was followed by several more popular Cloud 9/Sanctuary/Disney series for which I was fortunate to compose the music (much of it with Simon Lockyer).

I wrote the music and lyrics for 'Getaway' as the theme for *The Adventures of Swiss Family Robinson* starring Richard Thomas. The song was arranged and produced by the very talented Steve Mac, who has written and produced for Westlife, Leona Lewis, One Direction and James Blunt, to name a few.

The Tribe, first shown on Channel 5 in 1999, was one of the last major TV series created by Ray Thompson for Cloud 9/Sanctuary. It attracted a young cult following which still survives. The *Tribe* fans loved the title song, which I co-wrote with Simon and Ben Robbins, and we received a lot of positive reaction from them.

The international success of all of the Cloud 9 TV series I have just mentioned, as well as *The Legend of William Tell*, *Return to Treasure Island* and William Shatner's *Twist in the Tale*, gradually turned my ship round and took me, Rosie and the young ones out of the stormy waters of the nineteen-nineties.

This was not just in respect of my professional career and our financial security. During this period we were also coming to terms with the loss of my parents and Rosie's mother, which was a painful and lengthy phase in our lives.

By 1999, we were able to move from our rented home in East Horsley to a lovely Edwardian house in the middle of Guildford which, with the *Vorsprung durch Technik* help of my German friend Heiner and Rosie's clever artistic vision, was turned into a perfect family home for us all. We spent fourteen happy years there. Freddie walked down the road to the Royal Grammar School, and we had the pleasure of becoming the local B&B for all of Lucy, Olivia, Daisy and Freddie's friends after their partying in the Guildford pubs and clubs!

I AM sorry to disappoint you and my children but I can't and wouldn't even want to try to compete with those autobiographies of pop stars and celebrities who revel in their stories of 'Sex, Drugs and Rock 'n' Roll.' All I will say is that I threw away the 'Been There Done Cannabis' T-shirt many years ago at the end of one of my stays in New Zealand, which was one of the best decisions I have ever made in my life.

Most young people I meet in seminars or teaching situations will know that I take a robust stand against cannabis and other illegal substances and exhort them not to go there. I point out the consequences for the vast majority of us who have addictive personalities.

If I can succeed in dissuading just one young person from experimenting with drugs, I will have accomplished something to be proud of.

When I mention this subject to my students at Solent University (where I am a visiting Professor), I don't get 'preachy' about it. I just tell them that from my personal experience it's something I very strongly advise against. Not just because it's a major health hazard, but because it can also change your personality, create severe mood swings and has potentially frightening side effects like paranoia... oh and I can't remember the other side effect it has!

(Thought you might like to know that when I was writing this, I had to check the spelling of 'paranoia' on the internet and it said: 'Why are you looking me up?')

What's more, I tell my students that I believe you can enjoy life and be just as creative in your work without the stuff. Nearly all of what I consider to be my best music (including *EastEnders* and *Howards' Way*) was written 'clean'.

BY 2000 I was back writing music for the BBC. The title music from *Castaway* and *Animal Park* has another strong connection for me, as both these BBC TV programmes featured Ben Fogle (not forgetting Kate Humble, co-presenter of *Animal Park* which is still shown on BBC2).

I first got to know Jeremy Mills, Producer of *Castaway*, before he left BBC TV to co-create Lion TV. As I mentioned earlier, Jeremy directed the *People* episode featuring Melody and her performance of the 'People Like You' theme song, and we have kept in touch since then.

The *Castaway* theme is one of the few for which we were given a very precise and focused brief. Before any shots were filmed, Jeremy conveyed to my co-composer Simon and me the planned opening sequence, as the camera roamed over the water towards Taransay, a remote Scottish island in the Outer Hebrides. The dramatic moment as the camera reached the shores of the island was the moment for the main *Castaway* theme to be established. How I wish that more producers were able to know exactly what they wanted at first briefing!

Animal Park originally began as a documentary about Longleat Park before it was developed and given its new title *Animal Park*; again, we were fortunate to be given an accurate musical brief by the Endemol producers, an imposing classical feel which was to accompany a roving camera shot over the Longleat estate and house.

The end-titles were just a bit of fun combining pop and a classical chord sequence. As in my song 'Wolfgang', I have always enjoyed the blend of pop and classical music and this was no exception.

I am so happy to see the meteoric rise of many of my earlier BBC and ITV producers like Peter 'Baz' Bazalgette at Endemol (before leaving to new pastures as Chair of the Arts Council) and Jeremy at Lion TV. They were all, with many others, given the chance by new government regulations to establish and consolidate their own independent production companies and help to capture no less than 50% of the world market with their innovative TV formats, from which they were permitted to retain overseas rights, and which in the last year or so have collectively contributed well over a billion pounds to our UK balance of payments!

The continuing success of the main TV networks in partnership with the independent production companies is, in my view, an excellent business model. As long as the government doesn't dilute the notion of the BBC licence fee!

Step By Step

E DUCATION, EDUCATION... WITHOUT wishing to sound too dark I'd like my gravestone to have space enough to include all of the following: 'Husband, father, brother, friend, composer and educator'! That's probably too many words for a gravestone!

But I've always said more than less, as everyone who knows me will agree. My dear friend and agent/publicist Jackie Gill once replied to one of my overlong emails: 'Simon, when I got to your fifth para, I was nearly choking on a piece of toast... and for a few seconds I didn't fight it!'

I have been blessed to enjoy two parallel careers – composer/songwriter and teacher, and have always been a passionate believer in education and enjoyed working with young people all my life.

Until a few years ago, I worked part-time at the Park Special Needs School in Woking (and also earlier at the Bishop Reindorp School in Guildford, now re-christened Christ College). Jan Foster, a good friend of ours in East Horsley, who works at the Park School as a Senior Management teacher, invited me to visit her school for a day to work with the children. I was instantly hooked. The Head Teacher, Karen, kindly offered me a part-time teaching post after a five-minute meeting.

I learned so much about all the challenges of special needs children – autism, ADHD (Attention Deficit Hyperactive disorder), ODD (Oppositional Defiance Disorder), SLD (Severe Learning Difficulties), and much more. I worked there one day a week for about five years and still hold happy memories of the staff and the children.

I still chuckle about stuff that happened there. One day I was in the secretary's office when a call came through from the older brother of one of the students, who demanded to speak to his brother. 'I'm sorry,' replied the secretary, 'we can't put calls through to students in class time, not even from family.'

The brother wouldn't take this for an answer. 'Well this is f****** important. I have to speak to him.' The secretary transferred the call through to the Head Teacher. 'I'm sorry Rameez, we can't put calls through to students unless it's an absolute emergency.' 'Well it is an emergency,' he replied. 'My brother's got my f****** fags!'

One of my young students with SLD asked me towards the end of the last lesson in the afternoon:

'How long does it take you to drive to *EastEnders*?'

'About two hours,' I replied. 'Why do you ask?'

'Because you need to leave soon and get ready for the programme, Sir.'

I was slow to understand what Steven was trying to say. In his mind it was my job to go to the set, where the programme was being made, and perform the *EastEnders* theme live every time the programme was being transmitted.

I couldn't help laughing at this misconception, but this was a valuable impromptu chance to tell Steven that most of the music played on radio and also the programmes on television are 'pre-recorded' not live. In my English lesson the next day, this topic was developed into a discussion about the difference between 'live' and 'recorded'.

We even got into a deep debate about how 'real' everything we perceive is, and how everything is not always what it seems. 'But isn't the Queen's Speech on Christmas day live?' one pupil asked me. I was sorry to disappoint her with my answer!

And in case you think that Steven's misunderstanding was obvious to us all, even you would be surprised to know how many 'live' interviews on radio and television have been pre-recorded, edited (even 'de-um'd and de-er'd!'), and made fit for public consumption.

There was another occasion when I was taking a lesson in social skills. One of the student's tasks was to make a phone call to an outside organization (library, theatre or whatever), and get some information.

It was Georgina's turn to perform her task. She had to phone the local cinema and ask what film was being shown that day. She was very nervous and rather giggly as the moment approached, and didn't want to make the call in front of the class, so I agreed to let her go out of the classroom.

As Georgina was in a wheelchair, I asked her lovely friend George to help me take her out of the classroom to the outside corridor and dial the number for her.

Both students were by now in a high state of giggly apprehension. George was a delightful fourteen year old with a rather high-pitched voice and an infectious nervous laugh that made the situation become funnier by the minute. Georgina's face was getting increasingly red with apoplexy, and I was struggling to keep a serious tone during the proceedings.

We got outside. George dialled the number on my mobile phone which he then threw onto Georgina's lap like a hot potato. She grasped the phone and managed somehow to blurt out: 'Hello I'm a student at the Park School and need to know what film you are showing today.'

After a few more jumbled words exchanged in this phone conversation, Georgina looked at me in desperation. 'What did they reply?' I asked her. 'Flied rice,' she said, giggling. 'I took over the phone and quickly realized that George in his panic had misdialled and got through to the local Chinese takeaway.

The three of us were by now howling with uncontrollable laughter. All the teachers popped their heads out of their classrooms to remonstrate with me for disrupting their lessons. We never managed to complete the task, but I gave Georgina and George a course mark for at least trying their best, and we returned to the class room, where in the next contrasting English lesson George wrote movingly about his foster parents and the love they gave him, after he was moved from Council care to live with them.

I learned as much as I taught at the Park School, often lessons that crossed over into my life away from the school. I discovered that if a pupil was in a defiant mood, wandering around the classroom restlessly or even destructively throwing books around, it was no use giving an authoritative instruction to sit down. So I developed a strategy of letting a disruptive pupil choose to do what I wanted. 'James, I understand that you are finding this writing task challenging. No worries. I'd like to help you after you've sat down. You can choose where. There's an empty desk by the window or you can sit here next to me at the front. Where are you going to decide to sit?' Not 'Will you sit down please?' More often than not the student feels he is in control and is deciding to do what he wants. *And he will sit down!*

I have converted this strategy to my clients and producers and usually offer them two demos of my music to choose from. I don't ask, 'Do you like my theme?' but rather, 'Which of the two themes I'm offering you do you prefer?' It doesn't always work – and probably won't ever again if any would-be client of mine gets to read this!

Music commitments forced me eventually to stop working at the Park, but in 2013 Jan's husband Paul, who worked as an educational consultant for the Priory Group, popped in to our home near Guildford for a coffee. 'I know you don't do any more teaching Simon, but one of my schools very close to you is in need of a music specialist for one day a week. How about it?'

Unsted Park is a school for Asperger students, and I have always been fascinated by high functioning autism. So I agreed to meet Steve the Principal who invited me to visit the school for a 'try out'. As a result I have worked there since 2013 with their talented and dedicated staff and TAs (Teacher Assistants), giving one-to-one music therapy to some of the pupils, and I have been amazed to see how music has a calming and deeply beneficial effect on some of the gifted students. One minute, they are stressed and 'kicking in'. The next, they are absorbed and focused on learning keyboard skills or writing a song.

Much better than medication, I'd say, although for me the jury is still out as to whether Ritalin, used selectively and carefully, is a useful tool to help some ADHD kids calm down and focus on their work.

When my daughter Lucy was eight years old and in her last year at Glenesk School, and Freddie in his last year at Aldro, I composed end of year songs for them both. 'Step By Step' and 'I'll See You Again' are still performed at both schools, and 'I'll See You Again' is also performed at the Park School and Unsted Park, as well as a few '*Smike* schools' to whom I have introduced the song.

The writing of 'Step By Step' was one of those rare spiritual moments when I felt, as I have from time to time, that I wasn't actually composing but rather was being 'dictated to' by a powerful external force. Yes, a privileged divine experience, if you believe as I do.

I remember Marion Jeffries, the Glenesk School secretary, phoning me one morning and telling me that the new school hall was shortly going to be opened, and as a surprise to Sue Johnson, the Head Teacher, they would like me to compose a new school song to celebrate the occasion.

Rosie went shopping and by her return I had composed the melody and lyrics of the song which I sent over to Marion.

Lucy had recorded the original demo, and on the evening of the School Hall opening I had the joy of being with the parents, staff and friends of the school, who were emotionally moved as they listened to the lyrics and melody of 'Step By Step'.

Sue (who died from cancer at the tragically young age of fifty-seven), embraced the song and made plans for all the pupils to perform it at the end of Summer Term Speech Day. When the kids turned round to face their parents and families and sing after all the closing speeches, there was a truly collective feeling of deep emotion, which I understand still happens at Glenesk at the end of every school year in July.

I believe that 'Step By Step' remains a lasting legacy to Sue and her family. She was one of the greatest head teachers we had the pleasure of knowing and being close friends with. So I hope you can see that music and education have always been inextricably interwoven throughout my whole life.

I have strong views about education that some of you may disagree with. I am saddened by the constant interventions and changes which governments of both main political parties have imposed on the teaching profession in recent years.

Education shouldn't just be about national targets, proscribed curricula, rigid strategies, lesson plans, excessive paperwork and league tables. It should also be about inspiration, teaching the children honesty, good behaviour and courtesy, as well of course as literacy and numeracy skills and the other subjects that teachers feel are relevant to their students.

One of the primary schools where I spent a day recently at a *Smike* rehearsal and workshop was an amazing school. The hundred young students I worked with were delightful, courteous, happy, skilful, hard-working and 100% motivated. The school had received an indifferent Ofsted report just before my visit. Personally I would have given it an 'outstanding' grade. All I can conclude is that the Ofsted inspectors had an inappropriate remit and questionable terms of reference. There is a compelling case to suggest that in some (and I mean *some*) instances, Ofsted can come across as a bullying outfit and not fit for purpose.

I have spent many absorbing days in my Special Needs schools, as well as at Solent University where – thanks to an introduction to the Vice Chancellor by Grahame Sewell, one of my tennis club friends! – I work with the music students and an inspiring team of professors, lecturers and course leaders led by Paul Rutter.

I also visit and work with as many schools performing *Smike* as I can and encourage young people to 'raise the bar' and achieve excellence.

Mr May :) iz COOL

Dear simon thank you for teaching m piano by benedikt

I decided to write about simon
May because he teaches at our school.

I think he' is a great teacher since
He does lots of fun lesson and he is a good listener.

He is a good friend.

He doesnot talk about his music much
unless you ask him.

"I am very Sorry what I done"

"Sorry" Teacher & Stuff:

"A" I was very rude to Simon May I will promis
I will not do this to any teacher or stuff
I will will try to do my work in school
I will not swear to any one in school and
that is a promis.

Dear miss Eshwood.

"B" I wanting to say I sorry what happened in
School I now I was so rude to simon may
I Just want or say sorry and promise not
to do be rude again. I will try to do my
work and not Swear. I wont be rude to
any stuff as well.

Thank you
By Oliver

And my dad will not making in some day for the
mentor.

Four of the treasured notes I received from recent pupils

Enjoyable? Usually, but not always. Challenging and rewarding? Definitely. Every time an ex-pupil comes up to me in Guildford and says, 'Hello Simon,' I am reminded of Terry Wogan's wonderful story of the priest picking up stranded sea crayfish on the shore and throwing them back into the sea. 'You're wasting your time, Father,' a stranger came up and said to him. 'It's just a drop in the ocean. You won't make any difference.' The priest picked up another fish and threw it back into the ocean. 'Made a difference to that one,' he replied.

WHEN YOU have finished reading my story, I would like it to have been on balance a 'feelgood' experience for you. For this reason I have consciously tried to play down the 'bad and sad' parts of my life, unless they were the driving force behind one of my songs or pieces of music.

But at this point I have to tell you about the moving and sad backstory to the song 'It Hurts To Say Goodbye'. ㉑

I have, like you I'm sure, experienced and had to come to terms with the untimely death of a young person. At Kingston Grammar School we lost Neil, one of the stars of my Under 12 cricket team, in very tragic circumstances. This happened at the time that I was producing *Smike* in my last year at the school.

Also I still wear blue and pink wrist bands in memory of two young friends William and Tildy, not only out of love and respect for them and their families, but also as a constant reminder to myself of how fragile life is and how we should always try to get our priorities right – even if I don't always succeed in doing so.

At the Park School in 2003, we lost Michael who, like his best friend Georgina, was wheelchair-bound and whose death affected all the staff and pupils.

At that time we were working with Mimi, a young, pretty and talented singer from my home county Wiltshire. 'Ever Since That Night' was one of the first songs that John and I wrote for her and reached the UK semi-finals of 'Song For Europe'. I guess it was fortunate that our song didn't get through to the final as this was the year of Tony Blair's invasion of Iraq, when the UK entry (Jemini) received that dreaded 'nul points'!

A few months before Michael passed away, Mimi came to the Park School as part of her pre-TV semi-final promo tour, and more importantly because Karen and Jan at the Park felt it would be a positive and fun experience for the kids. After Mimi had performed 'Ever Since That Night' to the whole school, there was time for questions and Michael, sitting at the back in his wheelchair, put up his hand and asked her: 'Is Simon your boyfriend?'

Lots of laughter, as I was clearly old enough to be her grandfather, but Michael's question didn't come across as inappropriate, just unintentionally very funny.

Shortly after Michael's death, about a year later, John played me the music and working lyric of a song he had just been inspired to write. As Michael had only just passed away I found it comforting and cathartic to write new lyrics for John's melody 'It Hurts To Say Goodbye'.

One More Chance

I 'M A SUCKER for the glitz and razzmatazz of Hollywood, and the lyrics in the song 'One More Chance' are inspired by my visits to the great city of Los Angeles.

On one visit, during a lunch at the Beverley Hills Hotel in Hollywood, I had the delight of meeting and chatting for a few minutes to Dolly Parton who wrote one of my all time favourite songs 'I Will Always Love You', performed by my idol Whitney Houston.

Dolly is such a warm and genuine person. I didn't overstay the intrusion. In Hollywood you can go up to most stars, introduce yourself and have a nice conversation… but not for more than ten minutes. That's the protocol.

Dolly and I traded memories of musicians and producers whom we both knew and worked with. I had the chance to tell her she had written one of the greatest love songs ever, she gave me and Rosie a big hug and fond farewell, and left me with happy memories of a very special encounter.

'One More Chance' is the story of a young actor who fluffs his lines in his first Hollywood movie shoot, but is given a second chance by his producer. It's also a love song about being given a second chance by the girl you love. As I mentioned before, I so enjoy writing lyrics that have more than one meaning.

My first trip to LA was organised by my publishing boss Peter Phillips in 1976. I was with two other ATV Music songwriters and friends, Miki Anthony and Vince Edwards. Peter took us to a smart Chinese restaurant on Sunset Boulevard but I didn't really enjoy that first night. I was already missing my family and felt very tired, hungry and jet-lagged. So much so that towards the start of the dinner I found myself tucking into what I thought was a prawn roll, but which was in fact a hot towel that the waiters give you to clean your hands!

On a later trip to Los Angeles in 2008, I found myself at Venice Beach on November 5th: the orange glow lining the top of the still blue ocean and the last moments of LA sunshine surpassed any beauty I have ever seen before on Fireworks Night.

That evening, the cold pitcher of beer shared by Mark Greenstreet, Gary, Paul, Michael and myself was as satis- fying as the knowledge that our flight was over and the real journey begun... and the warm breeze was a differ- ent sensation to standing in the heat of Ripley Bonfire Night in Surrey.

I raised my glass to everyone with an inner happiness, knowing that Rosie had just climbed Mount Kilimanjaro and was happy for me to climb my mountains on behalf of Simon and John, my writing partners, and myself.

LA has always been one of my favourite and most interesting places. It is the city of angels, ambition and dreams. A sprawling melting pot of contrasts, the rich and poor, the hopefuls and the hopeless, the helpful and the helpless. Because so many movies have been shot in LA you are not sure if you are on a film set or in a real city.

There is a constant feeling of surreality. When I am there I always pinch myself to check if I'm dreaming or if it's for real. The truth is that it's a mixture of the two. LA is a giant bubble. You step off the plane, go through the eye of sharp and rather hostile Customs and Immigration officials and then enter the world of make believe.

The poseurs, the smart guys, the nice guys, the down and outs, the beautiful people, the weirdos and bizarre hairdos on Venice Beach... I could go on.

LA's multi ethnic diversity is summed up by the parallel universe on the ocean front, where two worlds co-exist side by side between Venice Beach and Santa Monica, a conflicting mix of the local musos, artists, dealers and 'alkies' who live a few yards away from the beautiful set racing along the boardwalks in the pursuit of a healthy lifestyle and good living.

Dinner in Santa Monica was half an hour's walk from Venice Beach. Anyone who has been to LA will be familiar with those cyclists, joggers and skate boarders who preen along the dedicated lanes. The sight of this and the ferry wheel in the distance on Santa Monica pier dulled the pain of walking with feet, sore from the new shoes that I had worn since the start of the journey at Heathrow.

We had all budgeted for this important trip. No turning left as you embarked on the Virgin Airways plane. No first class cabin this time – in contrast to the flights to New Zealand I enjoyed when working on the Cloud 9 film series a few years earlier.

The Gallery Pictures team of producers and script-writers had come out to LA to advance the green light for their two movies and had kindly invited me, as their composer, to join them on their mission.

When we arrived at the restaurant, which was one of the rendezvous for the American Film Market delegates, Paul ordered wine on our behalf. He pointed to the Merlot house wine at the top of the menu. 'Bottle of your top Merlot, please,' he said to our waitress, meaning the House Merlot at the *top* of the menu. The wine tasted great. 'What a bargain for $7, well done Paul!' we congratulated him – until the bill came. The wine was, as we were to discover, the top, as in *best*, Merlot of the restaurant. Three bottles of the highest priced wine the restaurant had to offer blew all our budgets in the first evening, and Paul was banned from ordering wine for the remainder of our week spent together.

Our hotel by the ocean Hotel Cadillac was very close to the Candle Café where Nancy and Anna, our two favour-ite waitresses, would serve us breakfast. 'What are you writing?' Nancy asked me as she served me my omelette, crispy bacon, toast and freshly made coffee. 'I'm writing about you,' I said, and she gave me a warm Hispanic hug.

I listened attentively as Mark and the Gallery Pictures team planned their day's meetings, then went to my room to phone home and check that everyone was okay. Mark and his team went separate ways from me that day and I set off for Sunset Boulevard to have lunch with the American Company APM, which markets KPM and other UK music library tracks in America.

Don't ever think of trying to walk from one part of sprawling LA to another. Even going by bus involves three or four transfers. So it's car hire or cab every time.

The lunch with Georgia and Edwina, two of the best music library agents in LA, was pleasant and productive. (Their UK equivalent is my good friend Farah Hasan who at the time worked for the English KPM office and had introduced me to Georgia and Edwina.) Obama had just been elected President the day before and we all raised a glass to his success. We also talked about various ideas for a new album that I might offer our UK publishers for them to market in America the following year.

A few days later I found myself having breakfast in Beverley Hills with John Landis. Simon, John and I had already completed the title music and main theme for the movie *House Husbands* which Gallery Pictures were planning to shoot in 2009. They had also acquired the rights to a new treatment of *The Rivals*, the eighteenth-century comedy by Sheridan, and had arranged to meet the iconic John Landis with a view to persuading him to direct the movie in the UK. It was primarily to meet John that Mark Greenstreet had invited me to fly out with him and the other Gallery Films producers.

I say the iconic John Landis, because as well as directing many big movies like *American Werewolf in London* and

Trading Places, he directed the Michael Jackson 'Thriller' video which is one of my all time favourite pop videos.

I have mentioned before that every time I meet an icon I freeze and find it hard to make conversation. It was the same with meeting John Landis. He did all the talking. All I could do was listen and be enthralled by the amazing anecdotes he told about his career and all the famous actors he had worked with in the past.

When John caught sight of our showreel CD which I had left discreetly on the table in the garden, where we were having smoked salmon bagels and coffee for breakfast, he turned to me and enquired: 'Tell me about *The Dawning.'*

⑬ *The Dawning* was a British film from 1988. Based on Jennifer Johnston's novel *The Old Jest*, it depicts the Irish War of Independence through the eyes of the Anglo-Irish landlord class. It starred Anthony Hopkins, Hugh Grant, Jean Simmons, Trevor Howard and Rebecca Pidgeon and was produced by Sarah Lawson. Alan Murphy, who died at a tragically young age, gave a truly soulful performance on electric guitar on the sessions at RG Jones Wimbledon. Of all the music and songs I have written, my score for the movie *The Dawning* is one of Rosie's personal favourites, and mine too!

'Well,' I began slowly, 'it's a movie score I wrote.'

He gave me an actor's quizzical look with perfect timing: 'No Simon, what's the *movie* about?'

After I'd managed to summarize the main plot he thanked me for taking the trouble to give him a CD of our music. I could already see that this was a highly intelligent man who didn't suffer fools lightly.

During that week in Los Angeles I learnt so much more about the movie industry. On the last day of our week's stay, I rose early to pack before breakfast and go for one last stroll along the ocean front. It was a fabulous clear blue sky day. Was this a good omen or perhaps one of those false dawns?

As I packed T-shirts and tracksuits as homecoming gifts for the family, I looked back at the past week – so many new contacts and meetings, a special friendship with the Gallery Pictures team and the hope of moving forward with *House Husbands* the following year. We had done our best. All we could do now was pray that 2009 would see the 'green light' and wait for destiny to unfold.

Neither movie actually got the 'green light'. But a year or so later, Simon, John and I wrote the score for a short movie which Mark did succeed in getting financed and produced.

All of Me

I HAVE ALWAYS BEEN drawn to the 'Classical Crossover' genre – if there really is such a thing! When my friend and producer Geoff Kershaw invited me to renew my collaboration with Don Black and write a song for a TV documentary about Dave Willetts, I jumped at the chance. Dave, as you may know, took the lead role of Jean Valjean in the West End production of *Les Misérables*. I still enjoy listening to his recording of 'We Love Who We Love' in duet with Carol Woods, which was released on his latest album by Stage Door Records.

When I give occasional after-dinner entertainment, one of my favourite moments is to compose a spontaneous improvisation based on the first letters of my guests' first names. The seven random notes of the scale from A to G which I am given create the melody of my tune. I have to thank Andrew, Angela, Adrian, Anthony and Annabel who on one evening gave me their names in a challenging sequence of five A's in a row, which I found very appealing and which I used later in the melody of 'We Love Who We Love'!

If you are musical and sitting near to a piano, play the five A's and you'll see what I mean! Although I did cheat slightly and played the first A in the lower octave!

I had been aware of the talented classical harmony group Blake for some time. Lisa Davies, their radio and TV publicist at the time, introduced me to them in December 2010 with a view to exploring the possibility of us working together.

When I met them with their manager Adrian Munsey at the Royal Festival Hall, while they were rehearsing for a concert in the evening, we retired to their dressing room and chatted for about an hour.

I had just left the MPA (Music Publishers Association) annual lunch at the Hilton Hotel, but although I was feeling tired this was my only chance to meet them, and I didn't want to miss the opportunity.

I had a strong hunch that at last I had found the right home for one of the earliest songs I had written with Simon and John, 'All Of Me'. We had always believed in the song and recorded it several times with performers like Shane Ritchie and my old friend Johnny Griggs (who had sung the *Eldorado* vocal version of 'When You Go Away'). There was even a Nashville recording. Then in 2010, we recorded the song with the talented Charli Rouse for inclusion in my album 'The Simon May Collection'.

For the previous two years, the song had become one of the most requested and loved wedding songs on the USA Wedding Central's website.

I was getting regular requests for the backing track and sheet music from future brides wanting to have 'All Of Me' sung at their wedding. In fact, four very good friends of ours had played the song at their wedding parties, and there wasn't a dry eye in the house as the two couples (on different wedding occasions I should say!) danced and swayed to Charli Rouse's recording of the song. The song was also performed beautifully by Charli at our daughter Lucy's wedding.

But now in December 2010 I saw the chance to record the definitive cut of the song with full blown harmonies. Blake were the ideal and talented classical boy band to record 'All Of Me'.

In their dressing room at the Festival Hall, there was an upright piano and I played them the opening verse and chorus of the song. They liked it very much and we agreed to record their version.

We recorded the boys in my home studio. An interesting experience. Ollie, one of the group's members, was educated at Marlborough College. I can remember many years ago when I played for Dauntsey's hockey first eleven against Marlborough. It was renowned for being the annual needle match and our recording session of 'All Of Me' all those years later had a déjà vu feeling about it!

At the end of the day the four boys delivered a stunning vocal performance and the final Blake recording was very emotional and moving.

Mark Greenstreet directed and produced a fabulous promo video with Blake on location in Cornwall.

The Royal Wedding was scheduled for April 2011. The boys had been plastered all over *Hello* and other magazines as the guys who knew Prince William and Kate Middleton, the future princess of the United Kingdom. Jules, the lead singer, was understandably reluctant to be seen as 'cashing in' on his relationship with the Royal couple but like it or not, the association between the Royal Wedding and 'All of Me' was unavoidable. Blake promoted the song on several UK TV shows as well as on America's *The Today Show*, watched by over 20 million US viewers.

The 'single CD' charted at Number 1 in the Amazon 'physical singles' chart for several weeks. Apart from excellent TV exposure it was played a few times on national radio but didn't get on the important MOR ('middle of the road') playlists so made little impact in the all important iTunes download singles chart. Disappointing for 'All of Me' – or rather for all of us, because with more airplay it would have undoubtedly been a different story, and I think we would have enjoyed a smash hit single. You win some, you lose some!

After that we recorded another two tracks for the forthcoming Blake album, but by then we were all ready to move on. Shortly after this period, Jules became one of the stars of the BBC1 drama series *Holby City* and the other three boys regrouped as a three part classical harmony group. I wish them all well and 'thank them for the journey'.

Years before working with Blake, we were introduced to another classical vocal group, the lovely and highly successful Celtic Tenors.

They recorded a great version of our song 'Non Siamo Isole' with the awesome Irish vocalist Brian Kennedy in 2005.

This was the lead track on their album 'Remember Me'. It was quite a buzz being at the Royal Albert Hall and hearing the boys perform the song live for BBC Radio 2's 'Friday Night Is Music Night'.

Originally we offered the song to the Celtic Tenors in its original Italian, but they suggested that we write new English words for the verses and keep the choruses in Italian. This resulted in a storyline of a man visiting the Bay of Naples, who falls in love while an operatic aria is emanating from the distance.

Although English is the most commonly used language in pop music today, I personally find that lyrics and classic librettos in Italian have a special and unbeatable quality. Italian is, after all, widely regarded as one of the most beautiful languages in the world. Listening to a Mozart aria in English may be easier for us to understand, but for me is a much less pleasurable experience than hearing the original libretto.

Although I speak fluent French and German, my Italian is limited. When Simon, John and I decided to write 'Non Siamo Isole', we wrote the lyrics and storyline in English, but were assisted by the professional translation skills of Allan Adams who came to our studio to record the vocal in Italian!

Allan is an exceptionally talented classical tenor whom we have used on several recording sessions. He founded 'Opera on a Shoestring' in Scotland and is now a member of the English National Opera. The generous way in which he interpreted 'Non Siamo Isole' was one of the most exciting recording sessions I have worked on. Allan is a real star, and I would love this track to catch on in the future and be picked up by a discerning radio producer!

We still love Allan's original recording because it is all sung in Italian. You don't really have to understand all the lyrics, as there are enough evocative words like *la solitudine*, *la musica* and *l'amore* for you to get the gist of what the singer is telling us about.

When You Are Beautiful

AS I MENTIONED earlier, I love writing lyrics as much as I enjoy composing the music for a song.

I've never been certain whether the music or lyrics are the most important ingredients of a song. I am reminded of my friend, the very successful lyricist Barry Mason, who tells the wonderful story of how he went to the gents cloakroom during an awards lunch and found himself next to a guy relieving himself whilst at the same time whistling the iconic tune to 'Delilah', for which Barry had penned the lyrics.

Barry couldn't resist saying to him, 'That's my song, you know.' The guy looked over and replied, 'I thought that Les Reed wrote Delilah.' 'Well, yes,' said Barry. 'He wrote the music. I wrote the lyrics.' 'I'm not whistling your lyrics,' came the reply.

I guess that both are an essential part of the creation of a hit song. In fact I would say that there are eight essential ingredients for a hit single: a memorable melodic 'top line', an interesting and memorable lyric, an attractive chord sequence, a great vocal performance, an excellent arrangement and production, a clear and sonically attractive mix ('hats off' to my two favourite mixing engineers Keith Bessey and Gerry Kitchingham), and an effective promotion and strong marketing campaign. Of these elements a great melodic hook sung over a memorable song title are probably the most important two factors. Despite the occasional flak that we took for Anita Dobson's recording of the *EastEnders* theme as 'Anyone Can Fall In Love', with Don Black's singalong lyrics, the song fulfilled all these criteria and got to Number 2 in 1986.

⑧

I AM sometimes asked when and how ideas come to me and whether for example I wake up in the middle of the night inspired with a melody or a lyric. My problem isn't being short of original tunes or lyrics. It's remembering them! When I was writing the lyrics to 'By The River', for example, it was the afternoon, and I was so pleased that I happened to have paper and pen on me. Otherwise I would definitely have forgotten some of the words.

However, in the middle of the night when an idea or lyric unexpectedly hits you, it's not much fun waking yourself up properly and having to write down your thoughts. But I am often compelled to do so, because although I try to persuade myself in my half-conscious state that I'll remember something the next morning, experience has taught me that I rarely do.

So in order not to wake up Rosie, I always have one or two sheets of paper by my bedside and quietly scribble words down in the dark... sometimes hard to decipher the next day, because after an interval of a few minutes when an additional thought occurs to me, I then write on the same piece of paper, upside down or over something I've already written! But that's a lot better than waking up with a blank sheet and a feeling of regret that something has been lost forever!

Being inspired with a musical idea as opposed to a lyric is different. Very occasionally, if a strong melody haunts me in the night I have to creep into the lounge where we have an upright piano and scribble the key notes onto manuscript paper.

I don't have perfect pitch but what is strange is that when I'm half asleep, I can guess what notes I want to play on the piano and discover I'm already in the right key and the notes I had in mind are the correct ones! Is this evidence that the unconscious mind has hidden powers that are still undiscovered?

Earlier in my writing career I took the view that if you couldn't remember something you wrote the previous day and needed to be reminded by written manuscript or a recording, then it couldn't have been a very strong melody. That's a delightful theory that I still half believe, but those 4 a.m. hooks do sometimes still need to be logged for the next morning.

What I do know is that I can always recognize when I have composed a special melody, because firstly I experience an initial emotional reaction (as happened with *EastEnders*, *Howards' Way* and songs from *Smike*), and also because I then find the melodies going round and round in my head for the ensuing days after I have been recording them in the studio.

If I'm on a train, I always keep the bottom right hand side of my diary free to write down top lines either as letters or on a hastily scribbled five line stave!

The most frustrating experience is when you are dreaming and 'hear' the most amazing, original piece of music in your head which you half-consciously know will have vanished when you wake up. But even if I did get up and try to record this sonic 'dream' I would have to be wide awake to handle the studio technology, and the dream would have vanished by then!

Occasionally I have been so excited by a musical idea in the middle of the night, that I do indeed get up, make a cup of tea and quietly record a rough take in my studio. But it's not a lifestyle I recommend, and a lot of writers, especially authors, will tell you that they regard their creativity as a job which they start at nine in the morning like any other normal worker!

I have a theory that one day, maybe even in our lifetime, scientists will have developed the technique of monitoring and recording our musical brain patterns and it will be possible to plug into the mind and convert the soundwaves into the actual recording you are hearing. Whoever invents that software will make a fortune!

Until then we, as writers, remain a slightly bizarre breed apart, with varying degrees of abnormality! In truth I would claim that I am not an extreme case. Not as extreme, for instance, as Dave Jordan, a dear ATV Music writer from New Zealand who would be at a party chatting to guests and suddenly beat his breast and exclaim that an idea had just occurred to him and he needed to be alone to write down his new song. There is a time and place for everything!

Using words in a playful and imaginative way can achieve amazing results in the way that we communicate, as well of course as it can in writing poetry, lyrics and literature.

So for example, if you believe that a client is wrong you can either express disagreement which can be confrontational, or you can visualise to them what is happening in a light-hearted way, so that they understand the analogy but feel less directly threatened by it.

If producers tell me they don't like my musical suggestion, instead of telling them they may be mistaken, I might ask them to imagine for a moment that they are in Savile Row and getting fitted for a new bespoke suit.

'If I am the tailor and you are the client,' I would say, 'even though the customer is of course always right, it is my job to offer you a different colour cloth to what you may have had in mind. Try it on. If you don't like it, that's fine, but I would be derelict in my duty if I didn't show you all the different designs and patterns that we can offer you. I have taken your measurements and observed your skin and eye colours and my training as a suit designer tells me that green is the right colour for you, even though you are asking for red.'

If at this point the client does indeed continue to see red, then I'll back off and give him or her what they're asking for. But at least I've had the chance to draw back from a heated discussion about who is musically right to a more light-hearted and hypothetical scenario about dress sense and colours, about which my clients and I probably know very little and would find less controversial!

BBC Producer Nick Handel, whom I worked for several times, always enjoyed that analogy. 'Right Simon, I am coming over to your studio to be measured up for my next programme please,' he would say. The TV themes we wrote for Nick included *Jobs For the Girls* with Pauline Quirke and Linda Robson; *Jobs For the Boys*, the follow-up to that successful series; and an emotional programme *The Search*, which helped viewers find missing persons and was rather ahead of its time by linking BBC1 with every local BBC radio station.

Over the years I have discovered another example of the power of visualisation.

I compare the targets that I have at the beginning of a new year to a football match in which goals have to be scored. Those goals are written up on my 'Goal Score' which charts the progress from the first approach of a producer or the first idea of a project to work in progress, and then hopefully to final acceptance and inclusion in a film or television programme.

Until a few years ago I even had a model football pitch in my studio which our artistic daughter Olivia built for me, in which each 'player-project' moved up the field as we reached the penalty area. When our music was finally accepted, the goal went up on the scoreboard and we returned to the halfway line, ready to score again. If a producer rejected our pitch and gave the job to his nephew, we cried 'Foul!' and claimed a penalty which the referee had missed. This light-hearted visualisation would keep our sanity and our willingness to forget what had just happened, so that we could focus on the next period of the match.

Imagery, analogies, metaphors and similes are powerful tools and an essential part of songwriting. How many hit lyrics can you think of without a single metaphor or simile? For every one you could give me, I could more than match with songs like 'Cry Me A River', 'Climb Every Mountain' and 'Love Is an Ocean'.

The challenge today is to create new and original imagery, because the old metaphors have become clichés. Paul Simon's lyric 'Bridge Over Troubled Water' is a superb example of how to turn a cliché like 'water under the bridge' on its head and create a truly original simile. Describing the water as 'troubled' is an inspirational bonus. The 'icing on the cake', you might say!

Rosie gave me one of the best ever metaphors for a song that I co-wrote with my friend Ben Robbins and which was recorded by Natalie, the winner in the Belgian 'Pop Idol' contest in 2005.

As well as enjoying a long and successful writing partnership with Simon and John, I have also from time to time collaborated with Ben since working with him when he was tape operator many years ago at RG Jones Studio. I won't ever let him forget the occasion when, after a late night session, he couriered a copy of my ITV theme *The Roxy* up to Tyne Tees Television, and when all the producers and executives had assembled in the boardroom the next day to review my demo, the cassette was played and they listened to… nothing. Thanks to Ben's oversight the cassette hadn't been copied properly and was blank. With my teacher's hat on, I instructed Ben to write a personal letter of apology to Tyne Tees!

Forgive me please for digressing. Back to the subject of metaphors!

I was outside our kitchen home in Guildford and heard the sound of something crashing. I went into the kitchen and saw Rosie leaning sadly over the kitchen sink, holding a precious tea cup that was a sentimental family heirloom. She was holding the handle and cup gingerly.

'Is it OK?' I asked.

'It's a bit loose but I can mend it,' Rosie replied. *'It's fragile... not broken'.*

Wow... I thought instantly. If a precious piece of crockery can be fragile, not broken, so can a human heart after the break up of a relationship. I took that metaphor to a songwriting session with Ben and a few months later 'Fragile Not Broken' was the lead track of the Number 1 selling album in the Belgian Charts.

One of my early songs 'When You Are Beautiful' ③ crammed five similes into one lyric! Maybe a bit OTT, but I quite like it:

WHEN YOU ARE BEAUTIFUL

You're *like a little baby*
that gives its biggest smile
to a passing stranger, and then forgets him
You're *like a child that runs*
to greet a new found toy
And then rejects it
And then forgets it straight away
But when you are beautiful
Oh God, you are beautiful
Yes, when you are beautiful
don't ever change, please stay the same
You're *like a lighthouse on the ocean*
that casts its beam on the open sea
then plunges it in darkness
You're *like a freak one day summer*
You're *like a butterfly in colour*
that's flying high before it dies
But when you are beautiful
Oh God, you are beautiful
Yes, when you are beautiful
don't ever change, please stay the same

Some Personal Favourites

NOT EVERYTHING WE write is commercially successful and I think this must be the case for every songwriter and composer. But you always have songs and melodies that remain in your 'A' list even if they haven't yet become hits.

By The River & I'm Drowning
'By The River' and 'I'm Drowning' are two of my personal favourite songs co-written with Simon and John.

When I was writing the lyrics to 'By The River' I was walking by the River Wey in Guildford and as usual had pen and paper in my pocket. I went with the flow!

I wouldn't have the arrogance to compare myself with songwriters like George Michael who wrote one of my all-time favourite lyrics in 'Careless Whisper' – 'Guilty feet have got no rhythm' – but I do rather like the lyric in 'By the River': 'Feeling sad in Cambridge made me blue...'

If you have ever listened to 'By The River', I wonder if you noticed the Cambridge 'Blue' connotation in the lyric before I brought it to your attention. I am very aware that the things we writers and composers agonise over sometimes pass over the heads of our listeners. We are understandably more attuned to the faults and merits of our work. Which has an upside and a downside! I'm not saying that we shouldn't seek perfection, because our reader or listener will (of course!) be discerning and instinctively know what's good and what's bad, but there are times when we should worry less. We shouldn't expect our audience to analyse and appreciate our work with as much intensity as we bring to it!

Just as a hostess serving her *pièce de résistance* at a dinner party might be nervous about the gravy being slightly overseasoned and at the same time hope her guests will appeiate the refined flavouring in her favourite dessert sauce, most of the diners will probably be unaware of such subtleties and just be enjoying a nice roast and apple pie!

The dangers of being an expert can often ruin our enjoyment of things. For this reason, when I have finished a song or orchestral mix *I try to review it like a 'punter'*… without fretting about that possible clashing note which is hardly discernable even to a trained ear! Not easy to do, which is why at Eurovision parties I never pick the winner and my 'non musical' friends always do, because they see the big picture… like the Bucks Fizz girls shedding their dresses or the stunning graphics of the Swedish artist who won in 2015! On the subject of Eurovision and the UK's lack of success in recent years I will spare you all my thoughts… except to comment that in 2015 the bottom four out of twenty-seven countries (including the UK) were four of the six entries which were not performed live or voted for in the Eurovision semi-finals. Mmm… you don't need a degree in statistics or psychology to work that one out!

Wolfgang (34)

Apart from our many holidays together, Rosie and I have always enjoyed going separate ways to spend time on our own. Rosie does all sorts of projects that are not for me or in my comfort zone, like climbing mountains and embarking on very ambitious charity bike rides with her mate Peter (married to Helen), whose company we always enjoy when we spend annual holidays in their lovely Majorca apartment

Many years ago, I took myself off to Salzburg for a truly memorable week to visit Mozart's birthplace and surroundings. I have always adored his music ever since singing tenor roles in *Cosi fan Tutte* and *The Marriage of Figaro* when I was at Dauntsey's School. I wanted to take in the history of his life, tragic as it was. I have always found it incredibly sad how such a genius and icon could end up in a pauper's grave. Thanks to the Performing Rights Society that wouldn't have happened to him if he had lived today!

When I went upstairs to the room in Salzburg where Mozart was born and cheekily ran my fingers over the keyboard that he had played on, I was deeply moved. During my week's vacation I travelled out to the mountains and lakes nearby, and stayed for a couple of days in the Park Hotel Billroth overlooking the lake.

I began writing the song 'Wolfgang', and on my return to England I worked with Ian Hughes who created a wonderful orchestration, incorporating some of Mozart's most well known works which I had chosen to form the backbone of the song. 'Wolfgang' is a mix of classical and pop and is, personally for me, one of my most favourite (and least commercial) works that I have ever had the joy of writing and performing.

㉟ *Glory Be To God on High (The EastEnders hymn)*
One of my most ambitious projects was to create a religious version of *EastEnders* using the lyrics of Barry Rose (the eminent organist and choir trainer).

I rehearsed several choirs including youngsters from our local school Glenesk and Holmewood House Prep School in Tunbridge Wells. Tony Pape, the musical director at Holmewood House, had been one of the first to produce a new version of *Smike* which was featured on *Opportunity Knocks* in the early seventies.

Again I used Robin Black's Black Barn Studios for the recording. It was complicated. We recorded all the choirs separately and built up a rich multi-track mix of voices, some very young and some more sophisticated choral singers. Again dear Ian created a beautiful classical orchestration and I commissioned a good friend Helen to produce a pop video of the recording which I believe can still be viewed today on YouTube.

I don't think that any of the young singers will ever forget the experience of recording the audio track and the video. BBC TV's celebrated *Songs of Praise* programme has also included 'Glory Be To God on High' in past programmes. This was without question a project to remember with great affection and happy memories.

Summer in February   ㊸

Every composer, including even Lord Andrew Lloyd-Webber, will tell you that much of their music was intended for one project but has often been re-used to find a different home. The score that John and I wrote for *Summer in February* is an example of this.

Although someone else was chosen to write the score for this 2013 movie, I have never regarded other composers as competitors, as athletes might do in an Olympic event.

I have many good friends who have written other very successful themes – such as David Lowe, for example, who wrote the BBC 24-hour 'rolling news' theme. (Such a clever piece putting loads of different chords against the *same* note of the BBC news beep!) Or Paul Farrer, whose music for *The Weakest Link* turned just four notes into a very distinctive and instantly recognizable theme.

My favourite metaphor to explain this feeling, is that I look at all of us writers as being fishermen or fisherwomen in a large lake. We are a long distance from each other and if one of us catches a big fish we offer a congratulatory wave from our boat, knowing that we were never going to catch the same one, as we weren't in that place at the right time.

Jealousy and envy are negative emotions and if we suffer from them we are the only losers. In showbiz, particularly, we all have to accept that you win some and you lose some!

Happily my sense of humour was quickly restored a few days after we didn't win that *Summer In February* pitch.

I had a conversation with somebody who had just come across one of my *TOTP* appearances on YouTube and she asked me 'Oh... didn't you used to be Simon May?'

Wow, that's a bit premature, I thought. There's still more music to write and more dreams to share with those I love.

To make matters slightly worse that same lady added: 'Gosh in that video you used to be really good looking!'

Was that meant to be a compliment? Guess you can take it either way!

Nothing Is What It Seems

EVER MINDFUL OF that lovely Wiltshire lady who asked me if I knew someone famous, I have always taken time out to be interviewed on radio and TV shows to promote my 'branding'. I especially enjoyed being interviewed on Radio 4's *Today* programme talking about the *EastEnders* theme being the most recognized piece of music in the UK, and when Evan Davis mentioned that I had also composed *Howards' Way*, John Humphrys, who was sitting at the large studio table preparing his next interview, looked up and said: 'Well Simon, if you composed *Howards' Way*, why don't you write us a theme for the *Today* programme?' I took him at his word and a week later was back on the show with my new *Today* theme. They only played it once during that second interview. A touch fanciful to think that the *Today* programme would have adopted it as their regular theme, but I framed the signed manuscript of my piece and sent it to them, and I believe that it is still hanging somewhere in the *Today* studio!

I also regard doing PR in the national and local press as part of my job. It's often quite fun doing press interviews, especially when it's with a journalist like the lovely Susan Hill of the *Star On Sunday*! PR in print often leads to PR on radio and television, because that's where the TV researchers trawl for the features on their programmes. I always send journalists an advance press release with any relevant information to ensure accuracy. A good professional journalist would never be insulted by any helpful facts and spelling.

As well as promoting the virtues of PRS on the BBC TV *Breakfast* show and *The One Show* and so nearly winning the vote of 'Top Celebrity' on Christian O'Connell's Breakfast Show (I wrote a special theme for him too!), I also have happy memories of joining the late Ned Sherrin on his Radio 4 *Loose Ends* programme. I still treasure a card which Ned sent to thank me for appearing on the show. It was a personally signed message with a sketch of Ned at the top. What a nice professional guy who obviously sent that same personal thank you to all the guests who had been on *Loose Ends*.

Grantchester

... Writing to a brief. The pitfalls.

I believe the hardest part of a composer's job is to understand and interpret the brief that the client producer gives – or doesn't give, sometimes.

When we are commissioned or invited to submit a piece of music or song to a producer, at the early stage of the commissioning process a lot of clients aren't really sure what they are looking for. 'I'll know it when I hear it...' is a comment I'm quite used to hearing, as well as the conundrums and contradictions that every composer is given. 'I want the theme to have lots of pace but dwell thoughtfully and gently on the hero's emotions...' Or: 'I want to hear sadness and joy, mixed with a hint of threatening violence and exuberance.'

What is even more challenging is that the goalposts often move from one creative meeting to the next. New requests suddenly ambush you from out of the blue as the producer listens to the initial musical responses to their brief and then changes direction, after realising that the first brief was not what was actually intended. Over time, I have got used to receiving unexpected requests, because the more often I take on a brief the more misleading – or perhaps I should say 'interesting'! – I expect it to be.

In one of Edward de Bono's books about 'lateral thinking', there is a fascinating page where the reader sees an image of a beautiful young woman.

Turn over to the next page and De Bono invites you to look again at the same picture, and what do you see after his prompting? An ugly hag! (Incidentally, the original picture, shown above, was entitled 'My Wife and My Mother-in-Law'!)

Our perceptions are often wrong and misleading. We often see things in a pre-conceived way, and then in a different light depending on how we are influenced and feel at the time. Life is a jigsaw puzzle, and it is only in hindsight and with time that we get the full picture. I have to remind myself constantly not to make important decisions too rashly.

I had worked before for Diederick Santer when he was Executive Producer on *EastEnders*. After leaving the BBC Diederick set up his own company Lovely Day with Kudos TV and in 2014 invited me to meet him to discuss the possibility of working for him and composing the music to a new thriller series *Grantchester*, which was about to be filmed in and around Cambridge.

I was excited by the prospect and when I met Diederick and his producer Emma Kingsman-Lloyd I thought we had an excellent chance of giving them what they wanted for the main theme of the series. I had studied in Cambridge, I knew Grantchester and the River Cam sprawling alongside it. I even went to the same college as the detective vicar who is the lead character of the series.

I visualised the opening sequence which required opening title music – King's College and the expansive lawns in front of the River Cam... the iconic image as we all know it... the detective vicar riding his bike along the backs towards Grantchester. I was seeing the beautiful lady in De Bono's picture. But the producers of

Grantchester were seeing the other face *even though it was exactly the same picture.* Their opening titles were set on the *other* side of King's College in King's Parade, much busier, full of pedestrians and cyclists, a faster pace, less majestic, less religious. The first piece that John and I wrote began with a beautiful Grace sung in Latin by Max, a young chorister from Kingswood House Prep School in Epsom who I had heard recently singing the part of Smike in their school production. What could better sum up a vicar living near Cambridge than a Latin Grace 'Benedic, Domine' that we and other undergraduates used to hear (and still do) before formal College dinners in Cambridge?

A beautiful haunting theme maybe, *but not what the clients wanted.*

After our second meeting with Diederick we now had a more informed picture of what was needed – a bustling, slightly humorous piece to accompany the detective vicar's bicycle ride from King's Parade to Grantchester. We and all our family and friends thought our second attempt was pretty stunning, but I think by that time the producers had moved on and found another composer. They had deadlines!

Failure and defeat help us along our journey in life, as long as we work out the reasons for that failure and learn the lessons from them.

'Dear Diary... Simon, God gave you one mouth and two ears. You must listen more and hold back from expressing a pre-conceived viewpoint, however passionate it might be.'

Since the *Grantchester* experience, I have become rather more reluctant to pitch for work. If a producer or director like Julia Smith and Tony Holland had faith in me and were prepared to share a journey of exploration with me and my team, well fine.

But if I'm in a restaurant and someone asks me to undo a stubborn bottle screwtop which won't open, I don't really want to be the one who exerts himself and after a lot of strenuous effort has to pass it to someone else at the table *(the next composer)* who effortlessly succeds in opening the bottle after I've done a lot of the hard work *(of establishing what the client doesn't want!)*.

As with the De Bono optical illusion sketch, I have learnt that first impressions and hasty interpretations of what we perceive can sometimes be good but often unhelpful.

In the early 1990s, while we were renting our temporary home in East Horsley after the concert tour, we had a sizeable sum of money which we decided to invest in premium bonds. Good fun and every month for a few years we would have the delight of receiving prizes varying from £10 to occasionally £500. But never the big prizes.

Just before buying our new home in Guildford, we cashed in the bonds which were earmarked to pay for the deposit on our new home in about a month's time.

Coincidentally, at the time we had to decide which school to choose for Olivia's sixth form education. Should she stay where she was, which was a distance away from Guildford, or look elsewhere?

I sent off the forms to the Premium Bonds office, allowing for the mandatory four weeks or so before we received the repayments.

Three days later our usual monthly prize money envelopes arrived. I opened them over breakfast and could not believe our luck. There were more envelopes than usual. Three payments of £10, one for an unusual £500 and two payments of £15,000!

After a few minutes of euphoria, Rosie and I immediately decided that we could now afford to send Olivia to our local independent school, St. Catherines in Bramley, where she would complete her sixth form education. She had lots of friends there and we knew it was the ideal school for her, which indeed it proved to be.

On that same day, we rushed to the school's end of summer term celebrations and Rosie dispatched me to the Headmistress of the school to see if any places for the next Autumn term were available. There was possibly just one place left and I used whatever charms and powers of persuasion I had to secure a place for Olivia. I wrote out the cheque for the first term's fees on the spot and enrolled her.

A few weeks later, Rosie came home and she still describes my face as being ashen pale.

I was still waiting for the premium bond repayments, had re-checked our receipts from three weeks ago and the penny had dropped. The £30,000 payments we received had already been sent to us much earlier than we expected and those two cheques of £15,000 weren't prizes... *they were the re-payments.*

Oops! We couldn't withdraw Olivia's enrolment and in any case she was over the moon at going to the school of her first choice. We took it on the chin and never told her until years later that we had taken on a financial commitment that we couldn't really afford.

So every time I receive new information or am challenged with a difficult decision, I now sleep on it, revisit it and keep trying to look at what I am perceiving in as many different lights that I can. Is the girl pretty or a hag? Is everything what it seems on first viewing?

This may sound obvious but I have also learnt that just as we can easily misunderstand something, we can also be misunderstood when the roles are reversed. Put simply, we can give out the wrong signals as much as receive them.

If you are a manager or team leader you have to be sure that the person you are communicating with gets the right picture.

If, for example, I am conducting an orchestra, I might want to rehearse a particular section of the music again. I could say 'Please can we start again at the repeat sign?' when there may in fact be two repeat signs on that page. Some players might assume, like me, that I'm talking about the last repeat sign. Others may only spot the first one on that page.

'The road was right, we must have read the signs wrong' (lyric from 'Every Loser Wins').

Or I could say 'Please can we go back to the repeat sign at bar 64?' which doesn't leave any room for ambiguity or confusion.

Going back briefly to our choice of school for Olivia, I don't have any strong doctrinal views about the pros and cons of state and private education. I have taught happily in both sectors and all our four children have been educated in independent and state schools and benefited in different ways from both. They are all well grounded and fortunate to have been well educated. At the end of the day it comes down to the quality of the head teacher and staff and which school is best suited to each student. Our class system is endemically linked to the two systems which is a great pity. So whenever I am involved in an educational project, I am always drawn to the idea of the private sector sharing its resources with the local community in outreach projects rather than advocating the abolition or punitive taxation of the private sector. If we forced the independent sector out of the system, the additional huge costs of educating all of the current private students would be prohibitive. Better to raise the bar in the state system, which I believe is happening in many of our state funded schools and academies today.

As a final comment on our *Grantchester* experience, I hope that Diederick looks back at our pitch and two meetings with positive memories. I guess I will never know. It's funny isn't it, that although we have clear memories of what we feel about other people, we are so often blissfully unaware of what they might think of us. Just as well really because if the truth hit us in the face every hour of the day we would find it very hard to get on with our lives.

I do remember some of my *faux pas* though. It was on the day of our wedding. Two of the guests were Donald Forbes, my former Headmaster at Dauntsey's, and his wife Tricia. They were close friends of my parents and joined me at the bridegroom's house to change after their long journey from Edinburgh.

I was dressed in my morning suit and making final preparations. I came downstairs to join everyone and greeted Donald and Tricia who were enjoying a cup of coffee and snack.

'The bathroom's free,' I said to Tricia. 'You can go upstairs and get changed.'

'I *am* changed,' said Tricia.

Mmm… how do you get out of that one?

'What I mean is…' I went on valiantly, 'you're not wearing your hat yet and there's a full mirror in the bathroom.'

Don't dig any deeper Simon. Just blush and try to brush off your blunder with a smile and shrug of your shoulders! People like you more for that.

I guess that all my friends know me for being clumsy and tactless, tactile as well. It is usually me who initiates the first kiss and hug and occasionally this can cause discomfort or amusement with people I meet for the first time.

We are who we are!

㊼ *Safe Haven*

Increasingly over recent years, the practice of TV producers commissioning music for their programmes with respectable budgets has declined. Only the high-profile drama series attract serious budgets.

'Oh sorry Simon, we've run out of money,' I often hear. Translation: Music is too often the last thing producers think about until the final stages of post-production!

Increasingly the business model for many media composers has changed. Writing what is known as 'production music' can make more sense. Production music is another way of saying library music. It is commissioned by a publisher and marketed worldwide to every producer and user in the television, film and radio industry.

The composer receives nothing upfront for the time and effort spent and often today even finances the recording of their work. Usually (on a 50: 50 deal), the publisher will then take care of all the future marketing and royalty collection. The music has an ongoing long shelf life, and although it may not appear to be as glamorous as writing for high profile movies and TV shows it creates a 'safe haven' for composers in a volatile and precarious world that we live in.

I have written many tracks for the famous KPM and Juice Music Libraries, also for Universal Publishing Production Music, De Wolfe Music, The Scoring House (run by the innovative Pete Cox and part of West One Music Group) and most recently for Beds & Beats Production Music where I am excited by the energy and commitment of Dave Bethell and his team who include Martin Webb and Farah Hasan, with whom I worked so happily when they were at KPM Music.

When I receive my quarterly PRS royalty statement, it is rather the same as seeing how your premium bonds have done, and it's fun and rewarding to see which pieces have struck lucky in any territory in the world. You get surprises and disappointments in equal measure.

Gone are the days when it was so much easier to create a hit television theme. There are several reasons for this. Firstly, the end-title music in a TV drama (as opposed to a movie) has a much shorter duration than it used to. The original end-titles of *Howards' Way* lasted nearly two minutes. That was before remote controls and multi channels had taken hold of our homes.

Today the TV schedulers are so paranoid about viewers switching to another channel, while end credits are being shown, that the end-titles last for a much shorter time. Presentation also has this rather annoying habit of 'squeezing' the credits and talking over the music.

Fortunately as our TV screens get larger, it is becoming easier to read the actors' and production credits, even when they do have to share the screen with images of the next programme coming up.

The only time that music is uninterrupted is when there is a very special episode of say *EastEnders* and the Executive Producer writes a memo to Presentation requesting that the credits be full screen and free of voice-overs.

I have a favourite analogy which compares the squeezing and talking over of credits to dining in a restaurant. Just as you are finishing the last mouthful of the main course the waiter comes up, snatches your plate away and thrusts the dessert menu in your face. When you have just finished watching your favourite programme and are still savouring and digesting it, do you really need presentation interrupting your enjoyment to advertise the next programme?

If You Have a Dream

I first started writing my musical *Rick Van Winkel* in 1999. It was first performed at my son Freddie's prep school Aldro and produced by Chris Powell.

As the show developed with changes and additions to the book by the acclaimed director and writer John Doyle, and later by my good friend Charles Garland, it was then performed at Feltonfleet School (produced by Chris Smith), Swanmore School at the Nuffield Theatre Southampton (directed by Mike O'Brien), the Eastbourne Stagers at Devonshire Park Theatre Eastbourne (directed by Dorothy Briant) and The Young Nomads Newmarket (produced and directed by Wallace Wareham). I give you their names because they gave me a lot of their time and talent.

Despite the support of a handful of good Surrey friends of mine and the stirling efforts of the Company's Executive Producer Richard Price, the show never enjoyed a full-blown professional run and commercial success. I am told that the songs, like the opening 'You're ㊾ Gonna Have a Good Time' and the closing 'If You Have a Dream', were stronger than the book, and the history of ㊿ musicals is littered with shows that never got the story right. Maybe one fine day I will revisit *Rick Van Winkel*

147

with the songs that I still love and go back to its original premise to find a way of making this musical work with a stronger storyline!

Sometimes you write for commercial reasons, sometimes because creatively you have to. Peter Coe, the original director of Lionel Bart's *Oliver*, once told me that you should spend half your career writing for money and the other half for yourself. If that's true, *Rick* until now definitely comes into the latter category.

In some ways, the opening and closing songs of this musical sum up my credo of having fun, but also having a commitment and belief in whatever you do – and whatever the outcome. My outlook on life is summed up by the lyric in the closing song 'If You Have A dream':

Your head in the clouds and feet on the ground
you're allowed to be free, that's how it's gonna be

Rick is a mirror image of *Smike*, and instead of flashing back to the nineteenth century, it tells the story of a young rebellious schoolboy who dreams of life in a hundred years' time.

Although he is a problem child who frequently misses school and stays at home in a world of his own, he is also a very talented performer and has been chosen by his teachers to play the lead part of Rip Van Winkel in the school play. On the afternoon of the final technical run through, instead of playing his lead role he stays at home in bed and dreams of being seriously injured by falling scenery in the dress rehearsal. He goes into a coma. When

he wakes up he is surrounded by a new family genera-
tions later, who are his new parents, brother and sister.
He sees the world in a hundred years' time with all its
amazing changes and dangers.

His two new evil cousins (who are played by the
two school bullies in Rick's present-day school) decide
to exploit him as a freak survivor of an earlier century,
because in the new era the world has been so swamped
by technical information, video games and deprivation of
individual thinking that everyone has lost the capacity to
dream. So the cousins plan to market his 'dream software'
as a unique app which everyone is keen to purchase.

Rick, the rebel, refuses to co-operate. 'Anyone can
dream, you don't need my help,' he tells his worldwide
television audience, and when the two cousins are about
to destroy him for his honesty and rebellion Rick wakes
from his dream. His cathartic experience has transformed
his attitude to life, and he rushes out of bed to the school
theatre to star in a magical performance of *The Legend of
Rip Van Winkel*.

Well, I thought it was a great story at the time. I still
do, actually.

Thank You EastEnders!

AT THE ORIGINAL recording session of the main *EastEnders* theme we also recorded a gentle, emotional variation of the theme which I titled 'Julia's Theme' out of respect and gratitude to Julia Smith. This version has been regularly used at the end of an episode when one of the main characters leaves the show – usually in a hearse or a taxi!

One regret I have always had is that 'Julia's Theme' wasn't used to accompany Wendy Richard on her journey from Albert Square, and I know that the producers at the time also share this sadness for an unintended oversight. Wendy was an extremely kind and down-to-earth lady and I'll never forget the genuine interest and care she showed our daughter Daisy on a visit to the Albert Square set years ago, when Daisy was already showing an interest in becoming an actor.

The current version of the *EastEnders* title music is very similar to the original recording of 1985. However, as I just mentioned, I have in the past been asked by some of the Executive Producers to re-arrange the theme.

We recorded a jazzy swing version for the 1988 spin off *Civvy Street*. Then in 1993 I was asked to create a completely different orchestration for which Johnny Griggs and I wrote new lyrics and arranged with a 'soul'

150

feel. The vocal version, 'I Will Always Believe In You', was performed by Sharon Benson and was well received by younger sections of the public.

However, the new soul instrumental version used as the title music in the programme received very mixed reactions from viewers. It was less direct and the main melodic hook was hinted at, but not played with such an obvious melody. The whistle in the ending coda disappeared, much to the irritation of several dog owners who wrote in to complain that their pet dog no longer howled at the end of the programme.

The high frequency of the whistle seemed to have a magnetic attraction for dogs, as well as for young toddlers who were drawn towards the television set by the sonic features of the original recording.

In 2009 Diederick Santer, the new Executive Producer, asked me to return to the 1985 version and create a cleaner version of the original, a bit like restoring an old oil painting. Simon, John and I used the original 1985 multi track recording by painstakingly converting the individual tracks into MIDI files which triggered new sound samples, similar to the original ones but improved sonically.

We recorded a new performance of the whistled melody in the end hook with Rowland Sidwell (then Custodian of the Guildhall Guildford) and blended it with the original synthetic whistle sound. The project was quite laborious and technical but the result is a new cleaner version of the original which is still used now.

The 'doof doof' tom fill was introduced for the first time in the opening titles.

In 2010 the Internet spin-off *EastEnders E20*, produced by Deborah Sathe, featured a new remix by Carl Darling who won a competition for the best contemporary re-mix launched on Annie Mac's Radio 1 show.

In the same year, 'Peggy's Theme' was commissioned by *EastEnders* Executive Producer Bryan Kirkwood who followed Diederick Santer before handing over the baton to Lorraine Newman and now currently Dominic Treadwell-Collins.

However, I reckon I've probably explored enough variations of *EastEnders* for now!

EastEnders is fortunate to have been in safe hands for so long. I have had the privilege and pleasure over the past thirty years of meeting and working for most of the Executive Producers (including John Yorke who, since leaving the show, until recently continued to nurture and oversee the series for many years as Controller of BBC Drama). They have all treated me with respect and consideration, something I never take for granted, in a tough and sometimes ruthless industry. For the past twelve years or so I also have to thank dear Beth Levison who, until the 30th Anniversary year in 2015, remained senior PA to the Executive Producer and always kept in touch with me with courtesy and affection, as have many others in the Production office like Jean Stevenson (now retired!) and Company Manager Carolyn Weinstein.

I won't forget a lovely long chat I had with Barbara Windsor who phoned me after she'd watched her exit from Albert Square, accompanied by 'Peggy's Theme'. She was deeply moved by the whole of that last scene in the episode and thanked me for enhancing the emotions of her departure from *EastEnders*.

Whilst on the subject of *EastEnders*, my pupils sometimes ask me if I get to meet the stars of the show.

Well yes, I have enjoyed meeting and sometimes getting to know many of the *EastEnders* cast over the years. The BBC has often kindly invited me to the various celebrations and parties that take place from time to time.

Letitia Dean (Sharon), Adam Woodyatt (Ian), Nick Berry (Simon) and Paul Medford (Kelvin) came to our home to chat about the forthcoming *EastEnders* music storyline in 1986. Adam decided not to join 'The Banned', as singing is not his forte, but he is a truly lovely guy and an amazing actor.

I have also had several delightful chats with June Brown (Dot), who is in my view one of the finest actresses on British television. She can do 'comedy' and 'poignant' at the flick of a switch.

It was also great to work with Shane Ritchie when he recorded 'All Of Me' at John's home studio, although we never actually got to release his version of the song. As well as Anita Dobson and Barbara Windsor, I have also on various occasions had the pleasure of meeting Gillian Taylforth (Kathy Beale), Martin Kemp (Steve Owen), Leslie Grantham (Den Watts), Perry Fenwick

(Billy Mitchell), Jamie Borthwick (Jay Brown), Nitin Ganatra (Masood Ahmed), Nina Wadia (Zanab Masood) Sid Owen (Ricky Butcher), Michelle Collins (Cindy) and many others.

I mention them all because without exception they come over as charming and nice people, without any conceit or pretensions, and have always been very friendly towards me whenever I've met them. Most recently, I was invited to Elstree to join the *EastEnders* 30th Anniversary and watch the live episode with about 600 or so other guests in the large BBC canteen, which had been decorated for the after-party. The atmosphere was electric! Cheering and applause at times, but at other moments you could hear a pin drop.

In the penultimate scene when Ian Beale hugs Jane, Bobby and Cindy there was spontaneous rapturous applause from the audience for Adam and his 'family', which culminated in a supercharged scene of emotion as 'Julia's Theme' was played over the 'big hug', followed by the camera panning slowly over framed photos of the Beale family and a montage of memories, as the music continued. The names of Julia and Tony were inscribed on a wall near the square and the allusion to the creators of *EastEnders* was both clever but also very poignant.

Executive Producer Dominic Treadwell-Collins, Director Karl Neilson and all the cast and production team came up trumps that night following a week of stunning television drama, watched by over 20 million people across the week. An impressive 12 million viewers watched the live episode, which should (as I write this in

March 2015*), receive loads of future awards if there's any justice. The following Tuesday's unforgettable episode culminating in Peter and Lauren's exit from the Square was also beautifully done, accompanied once more by my favourite section of 'Julia's Theme'.

After the live episode finished, it was celebration time for all the guests who were joined by the cast and production team, some of whom I already knew and others who I had the pleasure of meeting for the first time. I had warm conversations with many of the cast members… as well as the production team, scriptwriters and directors!

I won't dwell on all the conversations, but I particularly remember Pam St Clement being rather taken by the knowledge that I had only arranged the *EastEnders* theme in the minor key once – 'Pat's Theme', for her exit from Albert Square. Also Shane Ritchie recalling our recording session of 'All Of Me', and chatting about his son Jake Roche (who is the frontman for the highly successful band Rixton), and Eliot Carrington who gave a brilliant 'killer' performance as Bobby Beale that night!

And of course it was good to catch up again with Adam, Letitia and Gillian from the early days of *EastEnders*. Ben Hardy (Peter Beale) was great fun to meet too. We

⊕

---

* As I read the final proof of *Doof Doof* in summer 2015 I am pleased to have seen that my prediction came true! At this year's British Soap Awards, on 21 May 2015, *EastEnders* scooped eight of the fourteen awards including Best British soap, best actor and best actress, the three categories voted for by the British public. Thank you *EastEnders*, you are indeed the best soap on British television today!

had a photo taken of him, myself and Harry Reid (Ben Mitchell), and to my delight my female following on Twitter increased noticeably the next day as a result of him tweeting the pic! Tameka Empson (Kim Fox) was also delightful, as were Jamie Borthwick (Jay), Danny Dyer (Mick Carter), Jake Wood (Max Branning), Lorna Fitzgerald (Abi Branning), Ricky Norwood (Fatboy), and many others.

The whole evening was an exciting and memorable one for me, and I thank Dominic and his team for the invitation!

My Top Ten Tips

SOME OF YOU reading my story may not have a particular leaning towards music and just like reading autobiographies in general. Others of you, however, may already be studying music and have plans for a career in the music or TV industry. Or you may be passionate about music but are unsure how you can break into the industry as a songwriter, composer, singer or sound engineer. Or perhaps you may have a son, daughter or young relative who you wish you could offer advice to, so you can give them a better chance of becoming professional musicians, singers or writers. And finally, you may be one of my generation who has always loved music, but in your working life never really had the chance to develop skills in making or writing music. If you come into all but the first category above, well this is for you!

Before I conclude my book, I would like to offer you my Top Ten Tips for success, survival and happiness in pursuing a career or meaningful hobby in music... for what they are worth!

Tip No. 1: Find a reason for writing.
Remember that you are never too young or old to create music. I started when I was seven and I'm still writing and producing in my seventies! Remember that creating

157

music is the same as being physically fit. You have to practise regularly – every day, and even when you are on holiday feed your mind on music by going to a concert or listening to a piece of live or recorded music. If your ambition is to become a composer or lyricist, or indeed both, keep writing. But to maintain that discipline you need to be motivated and find a reason to create.

If you are like one of my students at Solent Uni, writing a song or instrumental piece of music may be part of your course work, so you don't need the Sammy Cahn phone call! There are however many other ways of finding a reason to compose. If you are at college and want to write music for movies, do some networking and make friends with the students in the film and media department. One of them may be making his or her first movie as part of the film-making curriculum. Offer to compose and produce the music! If you are a teacher, write and produce a musical for your school, probably in partnership with your Heads of Drama and Music (after you've performed *Smike* I would add!). If you can't sing well, then find someone who can... write songs with him or her, and promote local gigs where your songs will be heard, not locked in a cupboard!

Tip No. 2: Do not allow yourself to be intimidated by technology.
Even if you may have access to a recording studio in your college or neighbourhood, cancel your summer holiday if necessary, and spend the money on your *own* home studio. You don't need a dedicated room for this. Many

hit records have been recorded in bedrooms! Years ago it would have cost you a five-figure sum to set up your own studio. This is no longer the case. As I write this in 2015, an initial budget of between £1.5k and £2k is a realistic sum that you will need to spend to get you going.

If any of you reading this are not planning to have a home studio and are not interested in technical details, please skip the next page or so. Otherwise you might experience that 'Jackie Gill moment' when you lose the will to live!

You can for example buy an Apple 21.5 iMac computer (8 gig RAM) with an inbuilt 21" screen, and Logic Pro X software for around £1200. (The package includes a QWERTY keyboard and mouse.) If you prefer a portable studio, a Mac Book Pro is another very good option, but more expensive (around £1.5k)

As well as monitor speakers and maybe headphones of your choice (for anti-social hours and vocal recording), you will also need a good, 'weighted' MIDI keyboard with sustain pedal (for example a Studiologic SL990 Pro 88 note weighted master keyboard, costing around £300), which will connect to your music programme, with for example a Steinberg UR22 2x2 USB Audio Interface costing about £100.

The advantage of the Logic music software is that it includes a generous library of useful sound samples (drum loops, keyboard sounds, guitar samples, etc.) that you don't get with other software and have to purchase separately.

There are other MIDI recording software programmes like Motu Digital Performer or Pro Tools, which some composers prefer, but they are more expensive and don't include sound samples. I used to write with Dig Performer. I now use Logic!

A vocal set-up with microphone should probably be the second phase of creating your home studio, unless you are technically minded, in which case an inexpensive microphone (or an expensive Neumann) can be linked up to your computer quite easily. Do note that recording voices and live instruments is way harder than recording MIDI tracks!

You may need a stand for your keyboard or decide to position it on top of your control desk. Before making that decision, go to other home studios, look at the lay-out and decide what is best for your own set-up.

If, like me, you are not technically minded, or even technophobic, research everything thoroughly with anyone you know who is knowledgable, preferably has their own recording set-up, and is prepared to advise you. Write down a budget of all the costs and then add a 25% contingency amount. When you buy your studio equipment, also allow a small extra budget to persuade someone in the store where you made your purchase to come to your home and install the set-up and wiring, and then brief you on how everything is set up and works. Write down all the instructions you are given! In-store tuition is another option and will obviously be cheaper than home visits.

The 21.5 iMac computer can only be purchased direct from Apple stores, but you can then buy your control keyboard and accessories from any good dealer (like Absolute Music in Bournemouth, who are my favourite supplier. (Address: 855 Ringwood Road, Bournemouth BH11 8NE. Tel: 01202 597180.)

Personally I would prefer to buy my computer from an Apple store rather than online, as you will then find it easier to access practical help and backup.

I am told by Robin Black, who has his own studio, that when he recently *(March 2015)* bought his computer, the Apple dealer offered to give him instructions in store of how to use the equipment for a small fee of £75.

Tip No. 3: Be prepared to collaborate.
If you are technologically literate but can't write lyrics or top lines, then find someone to work with who can. Or vice versa. I have been lucky to work with creative people like Simon and John who are technically superior to me, but who are also very talented in all aspects of composition, arranging and lyric writing. We all bring a lot of everything to the table. However, some collaborations have more defined roles.

If you are in a band, decide upfront who is writing most of the material to perform and record. To avoid future contentions, try to agree in writing your commercial arrangements. You may decide that all members of the band co-write the material and jointly have a majority say in who will publish your songs. That's not always an easy one, as one or two members of the band may be the natural writers and not wish to share the copyright with the others. There is no absolute rule. I believe, for example, that Chris Martin is the main songwriter of Coldplay but each member of the band receives a 25% share of earnings. No wonder they've stayed together for so long!

In my last album for Beds & Beats I collaborated with six other writers, but I co-wrote the tracks separately with one or two of them and could never have been in the same room, writing all the tracks with six other composers at the same time. Unless you are in a band, working and touring together all the time, that kind of arrangement could never work.

As with the Beatles, every member in the group should be given the chance to offer material for the band to inter-pret, but it won't take very long to work out who are the principal creative driving force, and to ensure that the legal arrangements between all members of the band are fair to all parties.

If you establish a writing partnership with another writer, then you may do what Paul McCartney and John Lennon did, and 'co-write' all your songs together during that partnership period. Paul essentially wrote 'Yesterday' and John, I believe, wrote 'A Hard Day's night' but they were both co-credited.

It's not so hard to work out credits and an equal royalty share for separate composers and lyricists. (I wrote the music for 'Always There'. Don Black wrote the lyrics!)

You have to do what works for you and whoever you are working with. All I can say is that if you don't agree in writing who wrote what, before you start to enjoy commercial success, you will later fulfil the prophecy: 'Where there's a hit, there's a writ!'

Personally I have always taken the view that I'd prefer to share half the royalties with a collaborator whose talent helped to double them!

Elton John & Bernie Taupin, Rodgers & Hammerstein, Lennon & McCartney proved that collaboration often works best. You may be unaware that James Blunt co-wrote 'You're Beautiful' with Sacha Skarbek and another ghostwriter (Amanda Ghost!).

Tip No. 4: Cars don't have square wheels.
I wish someone had told me at the start of my writing career not to be afraid of using tried and tested chord sequences, instead of trying to discover a completely original one. Only the Beatles and a few other geniuses have done that! There are rules in songwriting that you ignore at your peril.

If an engineer is designing a new car, the wheels have to be round! You can't make good bread without flour and water! If a song doesn't have a memorable chorus, it probably won't go very far.

In your early writing stages, listen to one of your favourite songs that you wish you had written. Analyse its structure. What do you like about the song? As an exercise, imitate it and then make it your own. I'm not suggesting that you plagiarize, but before you express your emotions and musicality, know what the rules are before you start breaking them!

When Adam Faith, one of the biggest British pop stars of the late 1950s/early 1960s, made his first entrance past the doorman of the Savoy Hotel, he was formally dressed with jacket and tie. After several visits however, as the hotel staff got to know him and keep his favourite table for him in the restaurant, he started to dress casually. I guess he must have tipped well, but he was allowed to ignore the dress code which he had obeyed in the early days!

It doesn't matter what genre you are writing in: rock, soul, pop. dance, funk, classical... Listen to the hits that have been written in the style you want to write in, then 'go and do likewise'.

One of my favourite songs is Labrinth singing 'Beneath You're Beautiful'. The chorus has the same chord sequence as Take That's 'Back For Good'... and Wet Wet Wet's 'Love Is All Around'.

If you are composing an orchestral piece, a good structure is just as important. At the risk of generalization, you need a beginning, middle, a development section and an end. And also, as with a pop song, a certain amount of repetition. I believe that with instrumental music there is more scope for rule-breaking than in writing a hit song!

Tip No. 5: Write with honesty and from the heart.
When you are writing lyrics, try to be honest. Be original. Write about things that have actually happened or which you have personally experienced. Listen to what strangers might say on a bus or a tube, but of course only if they are speaking loudly and you can't help

overhearing! 'Mummy I want to go home!' a young child might be screaming. 'I wanna go home'... not a bad song title. Or you might hear someone come out with a cliché that you can turn on its head!

Some of the best songs have a storyboard. Some of the worst songs come over as a bland exercise in rhyming couplets. Nothing wrong in rhyming, in fact it's an essential ingredient in lyric writing. But the rhyming should flow naturally and not sound contrived.

All writers, myself included, do from time to time suffer from 'dry' spells, when nothing happens creatively. Don't fight it. If it doesn't happen quickly and naturally in a writing session, get out into the sunshine for a walk, jog, a game of tennis or whatever recreation appeals to you. Sometimes you do need to discipline yourself to meet a deadline, but we have to enjoy what we do for a living, don't we?

Tip No. 6: Record a demo of your song.
If you find the idea of setting up your own recording studio too daunting, dip your toes in gradually. Go first to a professional studio and pay for a demo recording of your song. The studio will no doubt at the end of the session give you tips about how to set up your own recording studio, and you can take it from there if you wish to.

Giving you a 'heads up', here are the contact details of good friends of mine whose studio and expertise you can hire for a few hours or a day. Their prices *(quoted in 2015)* will vary, depending on how much input you require from them. If you go with your piano or guitar skills and perform your own backing track over which you sing, that will be less expensive than asking the studio guy(s) to perform and arrange the backing track. Remember to limit the demo session to one favourite song you want to demo.

1. Mike Saunders (in West Sussex). Demo rates start from £250 + VAT (arranging playing/programming included). Contact: mike@mjsmusic.co.uk. MJS Music Ltd, Arundel, West Sussex. Tel: 01903 885563.

2. Ben Robbins Studio (in central London). Demo rates start from £250 + VAT, depending on time needed in the studio, and level of input (arranging/playing/programming). Contact: www.benrobbins.net

3. Robin Black (in Surrey). Demo rates start from £250 + VAT depending on time needed in the studio. Contact: robinblackmusic.com or robinblack321@btinternet.com

Tip No. 7: Back up all your work.
On iTunes you can create your own personal playlist of work you have recorded, and create an archive of all your songs and instrumental pieces. You should also invest in a dedicated hard drive on which all of your multi-tracks and stereo mixes are backed up. Back up everything in

more than one format (i.e. on a hard drive and also on DVDs which should be stored in a separate area to the studio back up drive).

When you are working on a new track, back up as you go – regularly, Very easy to do: you just press 'save' after every musical task has been done! This may sound very obvious to you, but I don't know any musician or composer who didn't lose a wonderful 'take' by forgetting to back up... once!

Tip No. 8: Find a market for your work by networking and presenting yourself well.

Perhaps more so than in any other industry, personal contacts and relationships are the most effective way to market your work. So network: go to live gigs, perform at gigs, join BASCA where you will have the chance to meet others in the music industry. But network honestly. By that I mean that you must like the people you are socializing with. In the words of *Desiderata*: 'Be yourself. Especially do not feign affection.'

Get publicity so that the industry is drawn to you just as much as you are drawn to it.

Go on Twitter, Facebook, Instagram and maybe LinkedIn. Create your own website. Put your recordings and videos on YouTube. But remember to get the balance right between your PR activities and the time and energy spent on making excellent music.

When you offer your work to publishers, managers, record companies or television producers, never submit more than two of your best songs or instrumental pieces.

They haven't got time to listen to more than five minutes of your creativity – *if you are lucky!* Here's the golden rule: 'Less is more!'

Take time to present your work attractively. If you set up your studio, it's worth investing in a small printer that can print on blank CDs with white labels, not those awful CDs which need to have separate labels stuck on them!

Sending unsolicited material in the post is a waste of your time and money. Period. I have never had work accepted which I sent in the post to someone I had never met.

There is absolutely no point in sending material to someone unless they have agreed for you to send it. In America especially, any unsolicited material is returned unopened with a disclaimer note from the Company's legal department.

If I had posted a CD of 'All Of Me' to Blake's record company, rather than playing it to them 'live' in their dressing room, I doubt if they would have agreed to record it... or even listened to it!

Nowadays I more often than not send my recordings online to clients and producers whom I know and who are expecting to receive something from me. 'Dropbox' is a neat system, because once the other party has accepted your invitation to download your files, you don't need to upload, once the system is in place. You just drag your file into the local Dropbox folder on your computer.

I personally use 'WeTransfer', as it is so easy to use. You go to the WeTransfer site, upload your files, type in the recipient's email address with a brief message, and your client will receive an email and link to enable a download. WeTransfer sends you an email to confirm your files have been downloaded. And it's all free, unless you upgrade to WeTransfer Plus which has extra benefits, like keeping your files online for more than a week.

Tip No. 9: Consider being managed.
When you have reached a certain stage in your song-writing or composing, consider finding an influential and honest manager. That is almost an oxymoron, but not quite! There are indeed a small number of fantastic individual managers who are well connected, effective and honest. But again, heed the wise words of *Desiderata*: 'Exercise caution in your business affairs; for the world is full of trickery.'

Some of the best relationships between managers and artists/writers have grown from an early stage when neither the manager or client had so far enjoyed success. They just got on well together and each had his or her own strengths. They built successful careers together. Coldplay is a good example.

Alternatively, there are many excellent established management companies that enjoy a long list of success-ful clients. I won't name any, as they probably wouldn't thank me for doing so, and also because different manage-ments are suited to different artists and writers. How you identify and persuade a top manager to represent you isn't easy. Personal contacts or encounters are definitely the best way forward.

It's harder nowadays to have face-to-face meetings with decision-makers. Security was much less tight when I walked into the Basil Brush production office at BBC TV all those years ago. There are nevertheless still social events and seminars you can attend when it is possible to go up to a speaker afterwards and introduce yourself.

I have never found the perfect representation, mainly because I'm probably not manageable and like to be 'hands on' in any given career situation. In another life I would undoubtedly have had more success if I had found the right chemistry between myself and the 'perfect' management. The lack of perfection I refer to is as much my challenge as theirs!

One effective way of finding a manager to suit your needs is to work backwards. Choose two or three artists or writers you admire… Research who manages them, then find a way of getting to know someone who works in that office. Probably not the top guy who will probably be unreachable, unless you are lucky. I can tell you now that if you tried to speak on the phone to Simon Cowell or get a personal email reply from him, it's not going to happen. Don't go to the other extreme, though. You can probably get to speak to the teaboy, but it's going to be several years before he gets promoted to a position of influence and be able to help you!

An alternative management situation is to find a good publisher who will promote and administer your copyrights. I've been lucky to have had plenty of those!

It makes sense that a third party can 'big you up' more than you can yourself… and can also negotiate less emotionally and therefore more effectively than you, the 'artist'.

Colonel Parker who was Elvis Presley's manager is reported to have said to one of the Las Vegas club owners, with whom he was negotiating Elvis's fee for a week's appearance at his venue:

'Well thank you for that offer which is fine for me. Now can we discuss Elvis's fee please?'

Tip No. 10: Learn how to spell 'No'.
The music and TV business is a tough industry. We all get many knocks and rebuttals. We have to get ourselves up after every setback.

I am certainly not claiming to have a surfeit of the following qualities, but we all need to strive to be resilient, sensitive, imaginative, self-believing, blessed with a strong sense of humour and brave. Not brave in the same way as members of the armed forces, policemen, nurses, firemen and amulance crews... but brave in a less physical sense: having a willingness to look a fool, be disappointed, take some risks and above all... yes, you know what my last piece of advice is: always remember that NO is spelt YES!

Conclusion:
I have never tried to calculate what my 'hit rate' is – that is, the ratio of success and failure. I often tell my music students that I wrote over two hundred songs and compositions before I had my first commercial success.

Obviously, since then my success rate has improved considerably.

Like everyone, I have made mistakes and errors of judgment, but I have also made breakthroughs against all the odds. I have enjoyed a number one hit in the USA (co-producing 'Knock On Wood' by Amii Stewart) and also in the UK ('Every Loser Wins' by Nick Berry), as well as writing theme music that thankfully remains in the hearts of many viewers. And to hear my *EastEnders* theme being played at the Opening Ceremony of the UK Summer Olympics 2012 to a worldwide audience of 900 million viewers is something to be proud of... As well as making a decent living as a songwriter/composer for forty years!

But should I have invested so much time and money in a costly concert tour and two other musicals that never made it? My East Horsley and other friends who backed *Rick Van Winkel* have never held it against me that they lost their stake in the musical. And Rosie has never held it against me that in the past I often dared to have a vision and go for it, even though it may have resulted in failure.

You may, by the way, have questioned why I have mentioned my wife so many times in what is meant to be *my* autobiography. Well there's a simple answer to that – if I hadn't, there wouldn't have been so much of a story to tell!

The two of us have taken enough risks and adventurous projects for a lifetime and we are now enjoying more peaceful waters. But I don't think that either of us will ever regret being fearless and always willing to go where others might have played it safer.

To quote US President Franklin Delano Roosevelt – Our 'place shall never be with those cold and timid souls who neither know victory nor defeat'.

Maybe in my earlier life I sometimes tried too hard and people smelt that hunger. If you want something too much it may not happen. I don't mean that athletes shouldn't push themselves out of their comfort zone or that aspiring musicians, singers and actors shouldn't rehearse for ridiculously long hours. What I mean is that when we sell ourselves, being cool and slightly laid-back can have better results than looking desperate and willing to do anything.

Here is, I promise you, my very last analogy: close your eyes in the sunlight. You will see a black dot in the centre of a hazy grey pattern that you are drawn to. Follow that dot and pattern and it will move away from you to the side of your vision. Stop following it, and it will come back into the centre. Lesson – don't try *too* hard. Relax and let it come to you, and you will probably achieve more than if you become so anxious that you will prevent success from happening naturally.

Making the right decision is something which only comes with years of experience, trial and error. If someone falls into early success, I would suggest that this will be hard to repeat because the reasons for that success will be random and not understood. Hubris can set in and the willingness to learn from failure will be excluded from the process of decision-making.

So… thank you for allowing me to go off on that last unmusical tangent. Finally, my special thanks for improvements to the text of this book, most importantly Michael Neidus, Jackie Gill, David Bellis, Simon Gurney, James Gorely, as well as Hayley Knight, Walter Stephenson and Tom Haynes at Austin Macauley. And a special big apology to those of you whom I should have mentioned in this book but haven't. Thank you for your friendship which I never take for granted.

Epilogue

DESIDERATA IS FRAMED in gold and hangs on my studio wall. It is my second Bible and I live by it…

I would like to leave you with some of my favourite lines:

'Enjoy your achievements as well as your plans'.
'With all its sham, drudgery and broken dreams it is still a beautiful world. Be careful. Strive to be happy.'

Recently I spent a day at one of my 'Smike schools' for a workshop seminar. It was Tatworth Primary School where David Knight, the Head Teacher who retired in the summer of 2014, holds the record for producing Smike five times.

In a Q&A session at the end of the day one of the ten year olds asked me: 'How rich are you, Simon?'

The teachers in the room looked at me slightly apprehensively, wondering how I might react to such a blunt but honest question. After a moment's thought I replied:

'I am the richest person in the world…'

There was an audible intake of breath and gasps of disbelief coming from the eighty or so youngsters… But they were waiting for me to justify and quantify my reply.

'I have the loveliest wife and four children and son-in-laws that anyone could possibly wish for,' I went on. 'Yes, I am the luckiest and richest person in the world.'

Desiderata

Go placidly amid the noise and haste, and remember what peace there may be in silence. ⟡ As far as possible without surrender be on good terms with all persons. Speak your truth quietly and clearly; and listen to others, even the dull and ignorant; they too have their story. ⟡ Avoid loud and aggressive persons, they are vexations to the spirit. ⟡ If you compare yourself with others, you may become vain and bitter; for always there will be greater and lesser persons than yourself.

Enjoy your achievements as well as your plans. ⟡ Keep interested in your career, however humble; it is a real possession in the changing fortunes of time. ⟡ Exercise caution in your business affairs; for the world is full of trickery. ⟡ But let this not blind you to what virtue there is; many persons strive for high ideals; ⟡ and everywhere life is full of heroism.

Be yourself. Especially, do not feign affection. ⟡ Neither be critical about love; for in the face of all aridity and disenchantment it is as perennial as the grass.

Take kindly the counsel of the years, gracefully surrendering the things of youth. ⟡ Nurture strength of spirit to shield you in sudden misfortune. But do not distress yourself with imaginings. ❧ Many fears are born of fatigue and loneliness. Beyond a wholesome discipline, be gentle with yourself.

You are a child of the universe, no less than the trees and the stars; ❧ you have a right to be here. ❧ And whether or not it is clear to you, no doubt the universe is unfolding as it should.

Therefore be at peace with God, whatever you conceive Him to be, ❧ and whatever your labors and aspirations, in the noisy confusion of life keep peace with your soul. ❧ With all its sham, drudgery and broken dreams, it is still a beautiful world. Be careful. Strive to be happy.

© Max Ehrmann 1927

Appendix 1: Selected Song Lyrics

THE FOLLOWING SONGS are reproduced by kind permission of my publishers and co-writers: details for each are given after the song title. The numbers in the margin relate to the track number in the 3-CD set *The Simon May Collection*, published by the Demon Music Group (BBC Worldwide) in autumn 2015.

③ ## DON'T LET LIFE GET YOU DOWN
(SIMON MAY/ROGER HOLMAN)
Sony/ATV Music Publishing (UK) Ltd

People think they see a mountain
but it's just a little hill
And the problems that surround them
are just the mood they feel
But dangers in the darkness
are only in your mind
Better keep your eyes wide open
Look around
Don't let life get you down
Even though the world might let you down
Don't let life
Don't let life
Don't let life get you down
If you think that you're a loser
you're never going to win
You'll never change your situation
unless you think
and then begin
So get up go on go everywhere
and clouds will leave your mind
Cos the only one to make it will be you
Don't let life get you down
even though the world might let you down
Cos dangers in the darkness are only in your mind
Better keep your eyes wide open look around
Don't let life get you down
even though the world might let you down
Don't let life
Don't let life
Don't let life get you down

Repeat verse 2 and chorus

BORN WITH A SMILE ON MY FACE

④

(ROGER HOLMAN/SIMON MAY)

Sony/ATV Music Publishing (UK) Ltd

I was born with a smile on my face
The whole of my life's been a pantomime
Born with the need to embrace
the life of a clown telling rhymes
La la la la la la la etc
I'm here to help your leisure
give you pleasure
crack jokes to please you
try to tease you
Make you feel fine
inject some sunshine
Make you feel good
I knew it would
I was born with a smile on my face
The whole of my life's been a pantomime
Born with the need to embrace
the life of a clown telling rhymes
La la la la la la la etc
Forget the politicians
Nuclear visions
The gloomy headlines
Official deadlines
Let it all go now
Let me show how
it's all so easy to stay with me
I was born with a smile on my face
The whole of my life's been a pantomime
Born with the need to embrace
the life of a clown telling rhymes
La la la la la la la etc

SUMMER OF MY LIFE
(SIMON MAY)
Sony/ATV Music Publishing (UK) Ltd

⑤

Drinking up the last drops of the summer wine
Clutching straws by the riverside
And I look into your eyes
and autumn's getting near
You were the summer of my life
You were everything to me
You were all a man could need
You turned my darkness into light
You changed everything in sight
You were the summer of my life

Instrumental

I gotta think what I'll say to you
And what I say I think it's true
Did it ever cross your mind
that I'll always love you
You were the summer of my life
You were everything to me
You were all a man could need
You turned my darkness into light
You changed everything in sight
You were the summer of my life

Instrumental

You were the summer of my life
You were everything to me
You were all a man could need
You turned my darkness into light
You changed everything in sight
You were the summer of my life

MORE THAN IN LOVE

⑦

(LYRICS COMPOSED BY SIMON MAY)

Sony/ATV Music Publishing (UK) Ltd

More than you could know
More than I can show
Thoughts deep down inside of me
It's hard to show how much I feel for you and me
More than in love
You're a part of me and the feeling's so much
more than in love
And it's hard to see how anyone
could say with pride
Never loved or tried
We've a different meaning in the words
I love you... I love you
More each passing day
More than I can say
All my feelings say it's right
Remember how I thought
I'd lost you on that night
More than in love
You're a part of me and the feeling's so much
more than in love
And it's hard to see how anyone
could say with pride
never loved or tried
We've a different meaning in the words
I love you... I love you
More than in love
You're a part of me and the feeling's so much
more than in love
And it's hard to see how anyone
could say with pride
never loved or tried
We've a different meaning in the words
I love you... I love you

(Repeat chorus)

183

ANYONE CAN FALL IN LOVE
(SIMON MAY/DON BLACK/LESLIE OSBORNE)
Sony/ATV Music Publishing (UK) Ltd

Anyone can fall in love
That's the easy part you must keep it going
Anyone can fall in love
Over the years it has to keep growing
Sun and rain
Joy and pain
There's highs – there's lows
We've no way of knowing
Anyone can fall in love
That's not hard to do it isn't so clever
Anyone can fall in love
But you must make the love last forever
Who can say love will stay
It's up to you don't hide what needs showing
Anyone can fall in love
That's the easy part you must keep it going
Everyone can fall in love
But you must make the love last forever more
How do you keep the music from dying?
Love falls asleep unless you keep trying

Instrumental

Anyone can fall in love
Life's more than that it's pulling together
Everyone can share the love
Where we come from friends never say never
Side by side satisfied
to stay right here in one square forever
Anyone can fall in love
That's not hard to do it isn't so clever
Anyone can fall in love
But you must make the love last forever more
Anyone can fall… anyone can fall in love

ALWAYS THERE ⑨
(SIMON MAY/DON BLACK/LESLIE OSBORNE)
Sony/ATV Music Publishing (UK) Ltd

Always there
Your love is always there
No sea could ever divide
the love we share
It'always there
clear as the morning air
As sure as winds keep blowing
love will be always there
You, you were worth the waiting for
You're all I need and more
I'd be lost without you
Always there
The feeling's always there
No distance could ever change
how much we care
Love's always there
Forever always there
Like dreamers, sky and music
Love will be always there
When, when a love is deep enough
Then, then you can sail through stormy waters...

Instrumental

Always there
The feeling's always there
No distance could ever change
how much we care
Love's always there
forever always there
Like dreamers, sky and music
Love will be always there
Love's always there
Love's always there

EVERY LOSER WINS
(SIMON MAY/STEWART JAMES/BRADLEY JAMES)
Moncur Street Music/Peer Music (UK) Ltd

We nearly made it
We nearly found the perfect combination
The road was right we must have read the signs wrong
And now it's all gone
But if we'd made it
could we be sure that it was for the better
Who could say we would have stayed together
Nothing is certain in a changing world
Every loser wins
Once the dream begins
In time you'll see
Fate holds the key
And every loser knows
the light the tunnel shows
will shine on you and all those who knew
we nearly made it
But suddenly we seemed to stop
and lose our way
But did it really matter anyway
For that was yesterday
And we must live for now
Cos every loser wins
Once the dream begins
In time you'll see
Fate holds the key
And every loser knows
the light the tunnel shows will shine on you
and all those who knew
we nearly made it
Stand up and count me
I know you're on my side
Shine down on me and those who believe
that we can make it

PEOPLE LIKE YOU

⑭

(SIMON MAY)

Moncur Street Music/Peer Music (UK) Ltd

Millions of lives
Ships in the night
We know that nothing lasts forever
But we should not say never
To people like you
People we'd like to meet who
once in a while will smile and tell the story of their life
to people like you people like me
people like you
Millions of lives
One of them shines
He was a dot on the horizon
Now it's not hard to find him
People like you
People like me who'd like to know
Where did a friend go last year
What did she whisper in his ear
If people like you people like me
People like you
Then you perceive the sadness in her smile
Once in a while she'll tell the story...

Instrumental

Of people like me
People you'd you'd like to meet who
live on the street or outside
where the sun has time to shine
on people like you people like me
people like you

Repeat double chorus

Instrumental to fade

MORE TO LIFE
(SIMON MAY / MIKE READ)
Moncur Street Music/Peer Music (UK) Ltd

Free to run like the wind on a summer day
Heart worn like a ring around the moon
And your eyes are ablaze
Reflections of time passing by
that remind you there's much more to life
than standing still
or running from place to place in the heat of the day
Just follow your heart and you'll see
there's more to life
There beyond the horizon there's another day
Far above the pain and fear you feel
the power and pace
the greatest sensation of all
There is much more to life than you'll ever know
The rise and fall
There'll always be you and me
We're moving as one
So follow your heart and you'll see
there's more to life
We all have our dreams
We all have our visions
But time after time we're faced with decisions
Which road to follow
How hard to fight
Then you wake up and see
that there's much more to life
Free in acres of sky on a summer day
And the fire burns with hope inside your heart
We are never apart
Reflections of time passing by
that remind you there's much more to life
So just follow your heart and you'll see
if you follow your heart you'll be free
Cos there's more to life

So much more to life
More to life

WHEN YOU GO AWAY ⑯
(SIMON MAY)
Universal Music Publishing Ltd

It was over before it had begun
And often love can go that way
And I don't blame you for your point of view
You wanted freedom, I wanted you
But when you go away
You gotta tell me where you're going to
So I can dream I'll see you once again
Or when you go away
I wanna hear you say I'm with you
Then I won't mind when you go away
You showed me places I'd never seen before
although I've often passed their door
And if I had the chance to live my life again
I know for sure I'd do the same
And when you go away
You gotta tell me where you're going to
So I can share your Eldorado dreams
The music's calling you, it's taken up your soul
And I can't share that part of you
And I don't blame you for your point of view
You wanted freedom, I wanted you

Instrumental

And all that glitters is never what it seems
'cos Eldorado's only golden dreams
And when you go away
You gotta tell me where you're going to
So I can dream I'll see you once again

Or when you go away
I wanna hear you say that I'm with you
Then I won't mind when you go away
'cos Eldorado's only golden dreams

STEP BY STEP

(SIMON MAY)

Moncur Street Music/Peer Music (UK) Ltd

Step by step into this world we go
Bless this school for all we learn to know
Thank you God for giving us the chance to come alive
to work and play together you and I
Step by step please teach us how to grow
Let today help each of us to know
that given love we all must live together side by side
to work and play forever you and I

Instrumental

Thank you God for giving us the chance to come alive
to work and play together you and I

I'LL SEE YOU AGAIN (LEAVERS' SONG)

(SIMON MAY)

Moncur Street Music/Peer Music (UK) Ltd

We are blessed to be standing here today
as another year is over
Through the seasons in the sun and rain
when we laughed and played
and learned and prayed

190

Those memories will never go away
Onwards and upwards we will fly
like a bird whose wings can paint the sky
Nothing can stop us reaching the stars
On a high we say goodbye
But au revoir means
I'll see you again
To the leavers now we say farewell
We will miss you in September
All that's asked of you is do your best
It's our Credo, it's our prayer
And nobody can take that dream away
Onwards and upwards we will fly
like a bird whose wings can paint the sky
Nothing can stop us reaching the stars
On a high we say goodbye
But au revoir means
I'll see you again

Instrumental

Well they say that life's an Odyssey
like a river flowing to the sea
So our special thanks to everyone
for your love and inspiration
Those memories will never go away
Onwards and upwards we will fly
like a bird whose wings can paint the sky
Nothing can stop us reaching the stars
On a high we say goodbye
But au revoir means
I'll see you again
I'll see you again

EVER SINCE THAT NIGHT
(SIMON MAY/JOHN BRANT)
Moncur Street Music/Peer Music (UK) Ltd

Everyone says I'm bad for you
But everything they say and do
won't stop me being next to you
We're standing in a line outside
The bell will ring and if I find
you're not with me I'm feeling blue
You are my dream, my love, my miracle
And miracles don't happen every day
Ever since the night we met
all of my life has changed
Never thought I'd feel this way
So tell me you're feeling the same
Ever since that night, ever since that night
When Juliet met Romeo
no one ever let them know
their love would end in tragedy
But they will never understand
that when I'm yours and hold your hand
it's not the same for you and me
You are my dream, my love, my miracle
And miracles don't happen every day
Ever since the night we met
all of my life has changed
Never thought I'd feel this way
So tell me you're feeling the same
Ever since that night, ever since that night

Instrumental

You are my dream, my love, my miracle
And miracles don't happen every day
Ever since the night we met
all of my life has changed
Never thought I'd feel this way
Ever since that night, ever since that night

Repeat chorus to fade

IT HURTS TO SAY GOODBYE

(SIMON MAY/JOHN BRANT)

Moncur Street Music/Peer Music (UK) Ltd

I never had the chance to know you
but you touched my life
Give you flowers and the dance I owe you
when I see you next time
I wish I took the time to tell you
all of those things I had to say
And all the pain and sorrow
will never go away
It hurts to say goodbye
I'm not ashamed to cry
to know the reason why
it hurts to say goodbye, it hurts to say goodbye
I wish I hadn't thrown that moment
that we had together
The precious time that I could hold you
will stay forever
I wish I took the time to tell you
all of those things I had to say
And all the pain and sorrow
will never go away
It hurts to say goodbye
but I'm not ashamed to cry
to know the reason why
it hurts to say goodbye, it hurts to say goodbye

Instrumental

I wish I took the time to tell you
all of those things I had to say

I never had the chance to know you
but you touched my life
It hurts to say goodbye
but I'm not ashamed to cry
to know the reason why
it hurts to say goodbye, it hurts to say goodbye

Repeat chorus to fade

IN THE WARM LIGHT OF A BRAND NEW DAY

(SIMON MAY/ROGER HOLMAN)
Sony/ATV Music Publishing (UK) Ltd

Today has come
I see the sun
It's shining everywhere
A change of heart has just begun
The silver lining's there
And when I'm feeling lost
I'll keep my fingers crossed
and try to show that I don't care
in the warm light of a brand new day
I found a long lost happiness
when I woke up today
The cold I felt inside of me
can now be pushed away
Cos when I'm feeling lost
I'll keep my fingers crossed
and try to show that I don't care
in the warm light of a brand new day

Instrumental with choral harmonies

For just one moment in my life
I needn't run away

This passing mood of happiness
will help me face the day
And when I'm feeling lost
I'll keep my fingers crossed
and try to show that I don't care
in the warm light of a brand new day

Chorus coda

In the warm light of a brand new day

ONE MORE CHANCE ㉗
(SIMON MAY/SIMON LOCKYER/JOHN BRANT)
KPM Music/Sony/ATV Music Publishing (UK) Ltd

Always knew I had what it takes
All I ever had was heartaches
The avenue of pain, the walk of fame
I wanna be back there again
Life goes on, the journey is long
But you saved my life forever
You gave me one more chance
And I won't let you down this time
cos you believed in me
And when the curtain falls
I'll turn to you and smile because
you gave me one more chance
Ever known a moment in time
when heroes either die or they shine
And every single frame that hits the floor
makes you wish that you'd given more
The show goes on
You have to be strong
But you saved my life forever
You gave me one more chance
I won't let you down this time

cos you believed in me
And when the curtain falls
I'll turn to you and smile because
you gave me one more chance

Instrumental bridge

And who would have known
that the day when you phoned
was the moment I needed a friend, I needed a friend
You gave me one more chance
And I won't let you down this time
cos you believed in me
And when the curtain falls
I'll turn to you and smile because
you gave me one more chance
You gave me one more, one more chance to live
You gave me one more, one more chance to breathe
  now
You gave me one more… one more chance to live now

ALL OF ME

(SIMON MAY/SIMON LOCKYER/JOHN BRANT)

Moncur Street Music/Peer Music (UK) Ltd

The first day that I met you
I think I always knew
that you were meant to be the one
And then the feeling grew
With God and friends my witness
our love will never die
I take the gift you gave me
Don't need to question why
For all the faults I'm made of
and all the wrongs I do
I'm not asking you to judge me

Just be true
All of me
is what I give to you
And everything I have
I wanna share with you
And with this ring
for all eternity
I make this vow
when I give you all of me
This life is short and precious
a one way ticket ride
I thank you for the journey
I know you're on my side
And we are only here once
I'm glad we shared this day
of knowing something special
that will never go away
For all the faults I'm made of
and all the wrongs I do
I'm not asking you to judge me
Just be true
All of me
Is what I give to you
And everything I have
I wanna share with you
And with this ring
for all eternity
I make this vow
when I give you all of me
All of me
that's what I give to you
And everything I have
I'm gonna share with you
And with this ring
I give for all eternity my love
I make this vow

Repeat Chorus

NON SIAMO ISOLE (WE ARE NOT ISLANDS)
(SIMON MAY/SIMON LOCKYER/JOHN BRANT)
Moncur Street Music/Peer Music (UK) Ltd

Io ti vedo
attravesando la piazza
Avevo il sentimento
che ci si conosciamo gia
Subito la
cambiavi tutta mia oh
Tutta mia vita il colore della vita
Non siamo isole
Bisogna essere
insieme sempre noi
Nessumo puo vivra senza
l'amore che sembra
per noi la musica
La sollitudine
un giorno che non resta piu
Non siamo isole
Te ne ricordi quando sorrivi
Io non sapevo che eri sui punto
di essere esser mio destino
E non ti fermi
come un fiume lungo al mare
Non siamo isole
Bisogna essere
insieme sempre noi
Nessumo puo vivra senza
l'amore che sembra
per noi la musica
La sollitudine
un giorno che non resta piu
Non siamo isole
Non siamo isole
Bisogna essere
insieme sempre noi
Nessumo puo vivra

La solitudine
un giomo che non resta piu
Non siamo isole
Un giomo che non siamo isole

WE LOVE WHO WE LOVE

(SIMON MAY/DON BLACK)

Moncur Street Music/Peer Music (UK) Ltd/Sony/ATV Music Publishing (UK) Ltd

We love who we love
And though the feeling's strong
Sometimes it all goes wrong
I guess luck plays the part
You love who you love
You can't control your heart
We love who we love
Can't help the way we're made
Who knows if love will fade
Don't think of that tonight
We love who we love
And hope we get it right
The choices we make
The chances we take are all spins of the wheel
It's not our fault for feeling how we feel
We love who we love
Most times the dream comes true
I'll keep my eye on you
Don't be afraid to start
We love who we love
So open up your heart
We love who we love
And though the feeling's strong
Sometimes it all goes wrong
I guess luck plays the part

You love who you love
You can't control your heart
The choices we make
The chances we take are all spins of the wheel
It's not our fault for feeling how we feel
We love who we love
Most times the dream comes true
I'll keep my eye on you
Don't be afraid to start
We love who we love
So open up your heart
Repeat.

③

WHEN YOU ARE BEAUTIFUL

(LYRICS BY SIMON MAY)
Sony/ATV Music Publishing (UK)

You're like a little baby
that gives its biggest smile
to a passing stranger, and then forgets him
You're like a child that runs
to greet a new found toy
And then rejects it
And then forgets it straight away
But when you are beautiful
Oh God, you are beautiful
Yes, when you are beautiful
don't ever change, please stay the same
You're like a lighthouse on the ocean
that casts its beam on the open sea
then plunges it in darkness
You're like a freak one day summer
You're like a butterfly in colour
that's flying high before it dies
But when you are beautiful

Oh God, you are beautiful
Yes, when you are beautiful
don't ever change, please stay the same

BY THE RIVER

(SIMON MAY/SIMON LOCKYER/JOHN BRANT)
Moncur Street Music/Peer Music (UK) Ltd

By the river you will find me
coming to terms with my destiny
And still water running deeply
helps me to find my tranquillity
Feeling sad in Cambridge made me blue
I just wanted to spend one more day with you
By the river you will find me
writing a song in the pouring rain
Then the suns shines and I'm happy
cos when it's all over I'll see her again
Watch the lillies in glory that live for today
Life is too precious, don't throw it away
On a mountain you will find me
coming to terms with eternity
And reflections in the valley
tell me that everything's meant to be
Tomorrow like rainbows is out of our hands
We're a drop in the ocean, one grain in the sands
By the river you will find me
coming to terms with my destiny
And still water running deeply
helps me to find my tranquillity
It's the beauty of nature that makes me feel sure
that creation's not random, there's got to be more
than a short life… than a short life
as I sat down by the river

(33)

I'M DROWNING
(SIMON MAY/SIMON LOCKYER/JOHN BRANT)
Moncur Street Music/Peer Music (UK) Ltd

There never seems to be a moment
when I have time to tell you
that I'm losing my mind
You hear the words that I'm saying
But you're not really listening
and I'm finding it hard
Why can't I get through to you
and make you understand
It's not about how much I love you
But it's about who I am
I wanna be someone I used to be
Why can't you see what's happening to me
I'm drowning, I'm drowning
It seems the world is on my shoulders
It makes me feel so lonely
even when I'm with you
I care so much about tomorrow
On ocean waves we're drifting
And the truth is I'm scared
Why can't I get through to you
and make you understand
It's not about how much I love you
It's about who I am
I wanna be someone I used to be
Why can't you see what's happening to me
I'm drowning, I'm drowning
I wanna be someone I used to be
You're the only one
who can help me
You're the only one…
I'm drowning

WOLFGANG

(34)

(SIMON MAY)

Moncur Street Music/Peer Music (UK) Ltd

I tried to chase a young man's dreams
I traced your footsteps on the stairs
The piano in the room where you were born
It seems to say they could have given more
A father takes you in the fast lane
where danger waits for those who dare
I saw the water in the fountain
the rush of youth and talent in the square
Why did you cry Wolfgang too soon?
Nobody was there to steal your tune
You said goodbye before you knew
there's more to life than music
You could have used it it like we do today

Instrumental

They made you go from strength to weakness
They never gave you any time
You never had the chance to live and love her
The deadlines took your peace of mind
You always travelled in the fast lane
where others would have never dared
I saw that water in the fountain
You could have been much longer there
Why did you cry Wolfgang too soon?
Nobody would dare to steal your tune
You said goodbye before you knew
there's more to life than music
You should have used it it like we do today

Instrumental

There's more to life than music
You should have used it it like we do today
And nobody would dare to steal your tune
You said goodbye before you knew

There's more to life than music
You could have used it it like we do today
Why did you cry Wolfgang too soon?
Nobody would dare to steal your tune
You said goodbye before you knew
You could have used it, you should have used it
like we do today
Auf Wiederschauen

GLORY BE TO GOD ON HIGH (EASTENDERS HYMN)

(SIMON MAY / BARRY ROSE / LESLIE OSBORNE)
Sony/ATV Music Publishing (UK)

Allelujah Allelujah
Glory be to God on high
Ringing out his praises from every steeple
Lord alone to you we cry
Give us goodwill and peace to all people
When you're down in despair
it's then you find His love everywhere so…
Glory be to God on high (Allelujah)
Ringing out our song of worship and praising
Lord of earth and sea and sky (Allelujah)
Songs of praise to you
Our voices are raising
The power and the glory for ever amen
In your care gentle dove
we live our lives in service and love
Glory be to God on high
singing and rejoicing from every steeple
Listen to your children's cry
Show us Your way
And peace to all people
for ever and ever amen

Instrumental

Glory be to God on high (Allelujah)
Ringing out his praises from every steeple
Lord alone to you we cry
Give us goodwill and peace to all people
Glory be to God on high
Glory be to God on high
Allelujah Allelujah Allelujah
Glory be to God on high
Ringing out our song of worship and praising
Lord of earth and sea and sky
Songs of praise to you
our voices are raising
When you're down in despair
it's then you find His love everywhere so…
Glory Allelujah
Glory be to God, glory be to God
Glory be to God on high Allelujah
Glory be to God on high (Allelujah)
Singing and rejoicing from every steeple
Listen to your children's cry
Show us Your way
And peace to all people
now and ever more

YOU'RE GONNA HAVE A GOOD TIME ㊾

(SIMON MAY)

Moncur Street Music/Peer Music (UK) Ltd

We want to make you welcome
You're gonna have a good time
We hope you have a laugh and have a lot of fun
You're gonna have a good time with us tonight
So take it easy

Forget your problems
And very soon you'll cease to care
A new world vision, use your imagination
You want the moon, we'll take you there
And if the day's been hard, not easy
well we've got news for you
You're gonna have a good time
You're gonna have a laugh and have a lot of fun
You're gonna have a good time with us tonight

Instrumental

So take it easy, forget your problems
and very soon you'll cease to care
The days are hard, so make them easy
And who needs school? I won't be there
You've gotta have a good time
You've gotta have a good time
while you're alive
You're gonna have a good time
You're gonna have a laugh and have so much fun
You're gonna have a good time with us tonight
You're gonna have a good time... yes!

(50)

IF YOU HAVE A DREAM

(SIMON MAY)

Moncur Street Music/Peer Music (UK) Ltd

Welcome to a new world, full of many surprises
There's so many things to see, to learn, to feel again
If you have a dream that you can believe in...
Yes, all of those things that you dreamed will come true
If you have a dream you can learn to believe in yourself
The world is your oyster, your wisdom the pearls
as the new world unfurls before your very eyes
Take the future into the past, make it last forever

There's so many things to see, to learn, to feel again
This boy has a dream that you can believe in...
that you think you've heard somewhere before
If you have a dream you can learn to believe in yourself
Your head in the clouds and feet on the ground
you're allowed to be free, that's how it's gonna be

Instrumental

If you have a dream that you can believe in
all of those things will come true
And if anyone says you're a dreamer boy
you can can tell them that they are too
The world is your oyster, your wisdom the pearls
as the new world unfurls before your very eyes

Instrumental

If you have a dream that you can believe in
all of those things will come true
So dream on...
All those things will come true one day
If you have a dream

Appendix 2:
Amateur Productions of Smike

O N THIS PAGE are the names of some of the schools and amateur dramatic societies and their producers and music directors whose recent productions of *Smike* I have personally seen. This has given me the pleasure of meeting the cast and production teams and sometimes even of working with them in a *Smike* workshop rehearsal.

My sincere apologies for any omissions.

If you click on '*Smike* productions' on the Smike website at www.smikethemusical.com you will find a more comprehensive list of all past productions in the last few years.

In recent date order:

- Little Sparrows Theatre (Adela Forestier-Walker, Susi Tenty, Sandie Hodges, Liz Coxon)
- Aldro (Tom Rainer, Lisa Hele, Jane Aldritt, Becca Toft, Jill Farrow)
- Tatworth Primary School (David Knight)
- St. Augustine's Priory School Ealing (Bridget Ogley & Kevin Allen)

- Kingswood House Epsom (Phillipa Watkins & Jon Marler)
- First Stages Devizes (Carole Berry)
- Rose Hill Tunbridge Wells (David Everist & Lawrence Wilson)
- Colet Court St. Paul's Prep School (Tom Foster & Philip Berg)
- Cranmore Prep School West Horsley (Richard Harris)
- Young Nomads Newmarket (Wallace Wareham & Simon Pearce)
- Durrington Theatrical Society (Julie Jordan, Joe Bunker & Mike Saunders)
- Losely Fields Primary Godalming (Asta Hodgson)
- City of London Freemen's School Ashtead (Sarah Chamberlain-Webber & Paul Dodds)
- St Martin's School Northwood (Mr M Singleton & David Tidmarsh HM)
- Ripon Cathedral Choir School (John Wright & Ed Spackman)
- Yvonne Arnaud Youth Theatre Guildford, Act Three (Ben Henson & David Perkins)
- Kingston Grammar School (Maggie Hannan)
- Brookfield Community School (Mike O'Brien)
- Nemcom Theatre Company Sutton (Pat Martin & Michael Morwood)

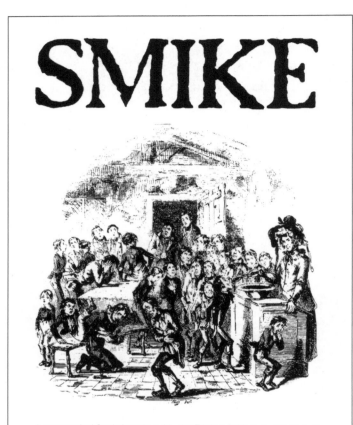

Front cover of the vocal score of Smike

Appendix 3: Tracks for the Simon May Collection

CD A

1 EASTENDERS
2 HOWARDS' WAY
3 DON'T LET LIFE GET YOU DOWN (from the musical *Smike*)
4 BORN WITH A SMILE ON MY FACE
5 THE SUMMER OF MY LIFE
6 WE'LL GATHER LILACS/ALL MY LOVING
7 MORE THAN IN LOVE
8 ANYONE CAN FALL IN LOVE
9 ALWAYS THERE
10 EVERY LOSER WINS
11 HOLIDAY SUITE (BBC TV HOLIDAY '86)
12 ITV OLYMPIC THEME '88
13 THE DAWNING
14 PEOPLE LIKE YOU 1988
15 MORE TO LIFE (from BBC TV Series *Trainer*)
16 ELDORADO – When You Go Away vocal version
17 JULIA'S THEME

CD B

18 STEP BY STEP
19 I'LL SEE YOU AGAIN (School Leavers' song)
20 EVER SINCE THAT NIGHT

21 IT HURTS TO SAY GOODBYE

22 CASTAWAY 2000 MAIN THEME (from the Lion TV/ BBC TV documentary series)

23 CASTAWAY 2000 REFLECTIVE THEME

24 ANIMAL PARK (Main Theme from the Endemol/BBC TV Series)

25 ANIMAL PARK (End titles of the Endemol/BBC TV Series)

26 IN THE WARM LIGHT OF A BRAND NEW DAY (from the musical *Smike*)

27 ONE MORE CHANCE

28 ALL OF ME

29 NON SIAMO ISOLE

30 WE LOVE WHO WE LOVE

31 WHEN YOU ARE BEAUTIFUL

32 BY THE RIVER

CD C

33 I'M DROWNING

34 WOLFGANG

35 GLORY BE TO GOD ON HIGH (*EastEnders* Hymn)

36 BARRACUDA (from *Howards' Way*)

37 ABBEY'S THEME (from *Howards' Way*)

38 FRERE (from *Howards' Way*)

39 HOWARDS' WAY (Reflective version)

40 PEGGY'S THEME

41 PAT'S THEME

42 EASTENDERS (Instrumental soul version 1993)

43 SUMMER IN FEBRUARY

44 GRANTCHESTER 1 (Demo of Main Theme 1)

45 GRANTCHESTER 2 (Demo of Reflections Theme 1)

46 GRANTCHESTER 3 (Demo of Theme 2)

47 SAFE HAVEN (KPM Music)

48 EASTENDERS ORIGINAL DEMO
49 YOU'RE GONNA HAVE A GOOD TIME (from the musical *Rick van Winkel*)
50 IF YOU HAVE A DREAM (from the musical *Rick van Winkel*)